No
Recipe

Also by Edward Espe Brown

The Tassajara Bread Book

Tassajara Cooking

The Tassajara Recipe Book

Tomato Blessings and Radish Teachings

The Complete Tassajara Cookbook

Not Always So: Practicing the True Spirit of Zen (editor)

The Greens Cookbook (co-author with Deborah Madison)

No Recipe

cooking as spiritual practice

Edward Espe Brown

SOUNDS TRUE

BOULDER, COLORADO

Sounds True
Boulder, CO 80306

Published 2018

Cover design by Lisa Kerans
Book design by Beth Skelley

Illustrations © Margot Koch

Printed in Canada

Library of Congress Cataloging-in-Publication Data
Names: Brown, Edward Espe, author.
Title: No recipe : cooking as spiritual practice / Edward Espe Brown.
Description: Boulder, CO : Sounds True, [2018]
Identifiers: LCCN 2017039564 (print) | LCCN 2017041464 (ebook) |
    ISBN 9781683640554 (ebook) | ISBN 9781683640547 (pbk.)
Subjects: LCSH: Cooking—Religious aspects—Buddhism. | Cooking—
    Psychological aspects. | Zen Buddhism—Psychology. | Gastronomy.
Classification: LCC BQ4570.F6 (ebook) | LCC BQ4570.F6 B76 2018
    (print) | DDC 294.3/446—dc23
LC record available at https://lccn.loc.gov/2017039564

10 9 8 7 6 5 4 3 2 1

No Recipe is dedicated to
Marj Burgstahler Stone

who called me out of the blue
more than ten years ago saying,
"I have your writing studio for you."

Sure enough—and that has made possible
the writing of this book.

Marj's life—and by extension mine—
has been greatly enhanced by the care
and loving attention of her daughters:
Brahna
Nichola
Melanie
Michele
Melissa

Love and Gratitude

You're the cook.

When you wash the rice,
wash the rice.
When you cut the carrots,
cut the carrots.
When you stir the soup,
stir the soup.

When you cook, you're not just working on food—
you're working on yourself,
you're working on other people.

SHUNRYU SUZUKI ROSHI

Contents

Before Words

A Meeting of Hearts

We meet again, here in the sweetness of our hearts,
where I might speak with you as though from inside.
I share with you a lifetime of experiences, teachings,
lessons; struggles, difficulties, joys, hindrances.
Though I have studied and practiced Zen and cooking
for over fifty years, I have no expertise to proclaim—
no recipe for you to follow.
Rather, I encourage you to find your own way in
the world
of food, cooking, and eating. To find your own way
of being you, your own way of expressing yourself fully.
Perhaps my stories will keep you company along the
way. Perhaps not.
Please see for yourself if my words are of interest,
and if you are drawn to reading further.
You're on your own.
Together with everything.

Reverential Offerings

*If there is sincerity in your cooking and associated activities,
whatever you do will be an act of nourishing the sacred body.
This is also the way of ease and joy for the great assembly.*
ZEN MASTER DŌGEN

Cooking makes love manifest. We tend a garden, head for the
grocery store or the farmers' market, receive the largesse of

food gifts from family, friends, and neighbors. We set to work or perchance to play.

Whenever food appears, it is the work of many people and the offering of other forms of life, a gift from Beyond, from sun, earth, sky, and water, from mystery. It is onion knowing how to *onion*, salmon fully infused with *salmoning*. It is blood, sweat, and tears; thoughts, emotions, and physical actions made visible, tasteable, edible. What we can put in our mouths, chew and swallow, digest, absorb, and eliminate has been sorted out from what we can't. It is offered, served forth. We go on living. Our bodies are nourished, and if we are fortunate, our spirits are lifted.

Ever since I was a teenager, I have devoted myself to cooking, yet there is no restaurant and there are no great recipes from my old-fashioned kitchen—which lacks oceans of countertops and acres of cabinets—where I prepare food for myself and my partner, Margot. Occasionally friends appear, and I offer sustenance. We share meals, and when the stars are aligned, conviviality permeates the room like the aroma of fresh-baked bread—which I sometimes serve. Our bodies are no longer protesting or complaining, magic is in the air, and all is well in the world.

Lifted, light, and buoyant with the sights, smells, and tastes of what is being eaten, the body remembers that it is also spirit. The divide between body and mind is bridged—no, the two are simply no longer recognized or found. They have become indistinguishable from the present, magnificently vibrant and awash with well-being. Whether spoken or not, *thank you* choruses throughout the room: to Source, to God, to the Divine, to family and friends, to the chefs, the growers, the pickers and shippers, to our ancestors, to the Blessed Ones and to those not so blessed, to all beings giving their lives. We give thanks. We are grateful. We forget ourselves. We forgive ourselves, and others. We praise.

It's in the cooking. It's in the eating, in the air, the ground, the sunlight. You can tune to it. You can bring it forth.

It's your good heart expressing itself, manifesting wherever you look. Loving what is. And using your body, mind, and heart to bring it to the table, ready to eat.

It's been a lifelong journey. I invite you to come along, at your own pace.

Envisioning This Book

I've spent way too many years aiming to write a book about food and cooking as well as about eating and eating with enjoyment. Though I believed it would be easy and straightforward, that was not the case. Not at all. Knowing that I am a Zen priest, people would exclaim, "Oh, you're going to write about being mindful in the kitchen." No, not really—as practiced, mindfulness in the kitchen may often be a hindrance. That is, in order to be mindful, you slow down enough that you become deliberate and exacting and eliminate any playfulness or spontaneity. No, I'm not planning to write that book.

Showing up and being responsive to the circumstances, carefully studying what's what, entering into your body's experience, following your heart as well as your head, moving into activity. Now we're talking my language.

Entering the unknown world of the kitchen may seem overwhelming. Yet we long to manifest our love in ways that nourish others. When we do not examine our assumptions, we think our cooking needs to be beyond compare, or at least beyond criticism. Will I tell you how to surpass others with your cooking so that you gain acclaim? Not likely. Perhaps you will learn to value your honest efforts.

Beyond this usual world of comparison proclaimed by the thinking of the dominant culture is the realm of spirit, and I would suggest, as many others have, that we are here learning how to bring this spiritual world to life in the material realm. We're studying how to share our hearts with others. Sometimes we hit the mark; sometimes we miss. It's a world alive with energy and feelings, with gifts from heaven and resources from the earth. You come into your own, reincarnating into your own life. Rarely do books speak of this: realizing your sacred nature and your capacity for genuine connection.

I want you to trust and develop your own sensibility, your own aesthetic. I want you to find and express your voice in the flavor, color, and texture of the food. Cooking is a lot like life. There is no recipe finally. Tentatively we follow the plans. Then we dream up what to do with ourselves, and the world.

I'm interested in encouraging you, empowering you to follow your own instincts, to trust your senses and your innate capacity to find out what you like.

I offer what I have to offer.

Love and Blessings to the Cooks!

At some point in the conversation I told her that the opportunity to study, to have life open up, didn't make an appearance on a rhythmic schedule. Because it doesn't happen with any particular regularity, I told her she had to say "yes," not to me, but to those moments. If not, then it wasn't just the opportunity in question that runs the risk of disappearing, but the idea of openness can also shut down.

KERRY NEWBERRY QUOTING ROBERT REYNOLDS IN THE *OREGON WINE PRESS*

In the course of writing this book I discovered that my friend and mentor Robert Reynolds had passed away and that there were several excellent articles online about him and his life as a chef, one that included the quote headlining this piece. I realized that I had been saying *yes* all these years and also found myself touched to have known this gracious, warmhearted individual who spent so much of his time with food—going to the markets, cooking, teaching, sharing, conversing—a man whose last book, *An Excuse to Be Together*, says so much (even in the title) about his sense for the place of food and cooking in our lives.

The man was down-home eloquent, and I found myself agreeing with so much of what he had to say: for instance, "The act of cooking ends in creativity but begins in the hands."

And much more than I ever have, he had joined in the flow of tradition, studying classic cuisine, especially French, yet could still sense the depths of being in the ingredients and dream up how to respond. Robert had an intimacy no matter where he turned.

Honoring Robert, I want to share some of the particulars of my way of cooking.

I buy decent, sometimes beautiful, produce, though I am not intent on seeking out the best.

Wonderful that many people and chefs are doing this and developing deep, abiding relationships with growers and producers. I have more Zen Master Dōgen's sense of using without complaint what comes your way.

Living in California I am able to have fresh greens, fresh vegetables, excellent meats.

My vegetables are often stir-fried to begin and then steamed to finish. One dinner I served seven different vegetables (one or two of them roasted, one or two blanched or steamed), each with a different tart element (lemon, lime, balsamic vinegar, pear vinegar, and so forth) and each with its own pungent element (red pepper, black pepper, garlic, ginger, mustard). I love seasoning with the tart and the pungent along with salt. What a feast! It's so delicious and without artifice.

My food is honest—that is, it's what it is, and you participate in the eating rather than having the taste without the texture. As cut surfaces release flavor—and I enjoy cutting—I slice my vegetables when I can into beautiful pieces, sometimes for instance slicing asparagus into long diagonal pieces that still poetically resonate with the shape of asparagus.

And I love to garnish, especially with fresh green: flat-leafed parsley, cilantro, and basil, occasionally fresh tarragon or spearmint, but also with green onion sliced in the elegant long diagonal strips of Japanese cuisine. Tonight, because my vegetable soup with chicken sausage got overly intense with chili negro, I garnished it with slices of avocado and a drizzling of lemon olive oil infused with fresh basil chiffonade.

I'm not trying to be inventive or on the cutting edge. I let things come home to my heart and let my heart respond. That's magic enough.

Love and blessings to the cooks!

1

THE WAY OF THE KITCHEN
Actualizing Sacred Space

The position of tenzo
(head cook) requires
wholehearted practice.

ZEN MASTER DŌGEN

I Will Always Be with You

I will always be with you.
SUZUKI ROSHI

In 1965 I met Shunryu Suzuki Roshi and began practicing Zen with him and others at the San Francisco Zen Center, which in those days was located on Bush Street in the city's Japantown. Though he died in 1971, I continue to follow his way and share his teachings. It is important, he said, to meet someone as sincere as you.

And he wanted you to blossom: "You think that I am the teacher and you are the student—that is a mistake! Sometimes the teacher is the student; sometimes the student is the teacher."

Once after a conversation in his cabin at Tassajara, he hugged me, which had never happened before. While he was holding me, he said, "I will always be with you." My body turned to light dancing up and down where my spine had been, and in the absence of a body, gauging my height was no longer a possibility. So I continue to sense his presence here with us—his voice, along with my voice, coming through me as I write. Most of my Zen teachers have departed from this earth, but they are living in the sky, in the waters of Tomales Bay where I sit writing, in the seagulls and pelicans. I invoke their presence here as well. We are in this together.

In 1966, after a year of practicing at the San Francisco Zen Center (most days going to meditation at five o'clock in the morning), I found a job at Tassajara Hot Springs, then a summer resort in the Los Padres National Forest, east and south of Carmel, California, where Bob and Anna Beck hired me to wash dishes. That summer the cooks Jimmie Vaughn and Ray Hurslander taught me to bake bread, along with the rudiments of cooking. Halfway through that summer, Ray quit, and the Becks asked me if I would take his place.

At twenty-one years old, the calm dishwasher became a temperamental chef. You know you're temperamental when you become the subject of group meetings called for that purpose alone: What do we do about Edward? And of course the primary responsibility for *doing something* falls to the would-be chef: Do you want to keep your job or not?

That fall Tassajara was bought by the San Francisco Zen Center, and I was invited to be the head cook, or *tenzo*, for the new, monastic-style community. Today it is pretty much impossible to understand how hard we worked. Several years ago, one of the Tassajara guest cooks asked me if I was ever a guest cook there. "Before you were born, yes, I was one of two guest cooks, and along with being a guest cook, I was the head cook, the head of student food, and the baker." Now each is a separate position, with four guest cooks and two bakers (and there are perhaps twice as many guests).

It just doesn't compute, unless you were there, how physically exhausting it was. If I was to sit down in the afternoon, I would fall asleep. Because of lack of staffing, it was often impossible to take days off, so I would work two or three weeks or a month without a break. And we were working in a small temporary kitchen while we built the new kitchen by hand—stone walls three-feet wide in the ground, eighteen-inches wide up the sides. We did construction ourselves in those days; now the Zen Center hires crews to come in and complete the building projects. The students meditate.

Most cooks have experienced incredible exhaustion, especially at the start. One chef friend of mine, who now heads a large dining room for a hotel in Südtirol, once spent three days working for an Austrian catering company in Dubai. Three fourteen-hour days were spent peeling baby carrots. "It's not natural," he deadpanned. "After two or three hours, you do not know what to do—whether to cry, scream, rage, or collapse—and you just go on."

When I was laboring in the kitchen at Tassajara, our teachers always said that work was a spiritual practice, not different from sitting in meditation. This was challenging to comprehend, yet I took their word for it and decided that I would cook as though I were doing spiritual practice—that is, I would put my whole heart into it and follow Roshi's teachings as best I could. Though dented by events, I survived. Time spent cooking saved me from some of the tortuous hours of sitting cross-legged in the zendo with painfully throbbing knees.

Slowly I was learning how to work as though the space, the food, the bowls and pots, and the counters and shelves were sacred.

Entering Sacred Space

Those without way-seeking mind will not have good results, in spite of their efforts.
ZEN MASTER DŌGEN

Working in the present can help shift one's awareness from past hindrances and traumas. Awakening to the world of today, you work in sacred space. Space where you can learn and grow rather than be graded on your performance. Space where, even before you start, you are loved and appreciated rather than seen as "less than." Space where instead of doing what's required (or else!), you generously offer your efforts for the benefit of family, of friends, for the benefit of what is larger.

What would make cooking a spiritual practice rather than mere work is cultivating a sense for what is sacred and doing your best to bring that alive in the world of the kitchen. Suzuki Roshi brought this to light by asking us, "What is your inmost request?" While some traditions seem to be rather specific about what is spiritual, here the sense is "to turn your light inward" and find out for yourself.

Please know I am not trying to tell you or anyone the right way to cook or to live—as though I knew better than you how to live your life. Each of us finds the way for ourselves. There is no recipe. If you're interested in navigating your inner world and connecting your inner world with the outer world, then you may find some helpful material here. You'll see pretty quickly.

Kitchen work tends to be demanding; as there is much to do and as (hungry) people want their food (already!), so much of my effort has been studying how to live in the moment—responding to its demands—with focus, integrity, and good-heartedness. This study has been informed by observing others skilled in the kitchen, reading books, listening to lectures, and most importantly awakening beginner's mind—seeing what you can find out rather than aiming for great accomplishment. Especially engaging for me as a Zen practitioner have been the writings of Zen Master Dōgen, particularly his *Tenzo Kyōkun: Instructions for the Cook*. So I will be quoting him from time to time.

Poetry speaks to me as well, so certainly it finds its way into the book. Finding language that speaks to us is pivotally important in our lives. You'll find out whether my language speaks to you and moves you on your life journey. When the words from outside resonate as though they are from inside, you know you've found a positive connection. See what you notice.

I'm not particularly good at setting down rules or guidelines or producing orderly constructs, but if you take to the story, you might well find it enjoyable and engaging. If my words are not speaking to you, by all means set them aside and find some that do—or write your own.

Making Sacred Space Manifest

Once when Pao Fu and Ch'ang Ch'ing were wandering in the mountains, Pao Fu pointed with his hand and said, "Right here is the summit of the mystic peak." Ch'ang Ch'ing said, "Indeed it is. What a pity."

CASE 23, *THE BLUE CLIFF RECORD*

Entering the sacred space of the kitchen, we don't know what will happen. We shift from the preoccupation of being in control to the focus of being in connection. Perhaps we breeze, our sails filling with gracious winds: flavorful food appears, and we hum with satisfaction and pleasure. Perhaps we flounder: the rice crunchy, vegetables mushy and dull-colored, the food outspoken in its refusal to match our pictures of delicious or even acceptable. So it is that we are in the soup, and while we strive to nourish ourselves and others with food, we do not always succeed. There is so much to figure out, from a workable (whether simple or elegant) menu plan (that does not have everything coming out of the oven or too many dishes on the stovetop at the last minute), to cooking times. There is so much to do—shopping, unloading the car, putting things away, cooking, cleaning up, the compost, trash, recycling—and so much to handle—ingredients, pots, pans, knives, dishes, leftovers, spills. One remembers Psyche given the task of sorting out a huge pile of wheat, barley, poppy seeds, chickpeas, lentils, and beans and how aided by an army of ants, she completes the assignment overnight. It's her ant-mind that she never knew she had.

In sacred space, help is available—and we learn to ask for it.

Speaking from the perspective of my Zen background, doing spiritual practice in the kitchen means taking up the task of creating this sacred space. Of course, sacred space is here all the time, as Pao Fu points out in the introductory quote. It's right here, so we do not literally create it as much as we embody it or practice it, so that our life is infused by it. We practice showing up.

We start by acknowledging as Ch'ang Ch'ing did, "Indeed it is." As different traditions have various sensibilities about what constitutes sacred space, along with how to acknowledge it and bring it alive—ways which are often powerful and trustworthy—I do not mean that Zen is the only way or the best way to do this, but simply that it is one you may find useful, as I have.

Which space are you walking in, working in? Ordinary space or sacred space? In ordinary space, we often feel caught up in circumstances as we face the demands of the day, which come along with performance standards or expectations, evaluations, assessments. We may sense that we are being judged, and we anxiously await the latest edition of our ratings. We wonder, can we get to a better place than here, where things seem so uncertain and unsafe, where struggle and stress seem constant? One answer people arrive at, of course, is to stay out of the kitchen—in fact, far, far away!

In ordinary space, we confront what seem to be established criteria for what is better and what is worse. Nothing lasts, so we remain at the mercy of shifting circumstances. Although our cooking skills may improve and we may receive more compliments, we know that our ratings could plummet at any moment.

In a further story about the summit of the mystic peak, Zen Master Joshu was asked, "How do I get to the summit of the mystic peak?" and his response was, "I won't say." When the monk pressed him, asking, "Why won't you say?" Joshu said, "If I told you, you would go right on thinking that you are now on level ground."

Do we live in a profane world, or do we say, "Yes, indeed, sacred space is right here"? Where are we? Awakening the mind that *seeks the way* to learn, to grow, to study, to investigate, already we are shifting into sacred space. Something could come through us.

Instead of aiming to go somewhere else, where everything is so much better, the Zen imperative is to recognize that the sacred is here by practicing, living, cooking in the way of sacred space. *No Recipe* is about how to do this.

This is not a book giving you instructions for how to make improvements in the everyday world or how to produce food that comes out the way it should (though it might), but one offering teachings for bringing alive your own source of sacredness. You'll find that your health, happiness, and well-being are less dependent on performing to or surpassing the outer standards of acceptability and more about trusting, knowing, and sharing your innate true nature. You yourself are worthy, wise, and compassionate, and you can bring that to life in the kitchen and out and about. You *practice making sincere and wholehearted effort.* You *do not think with ordinary mind,* and you *do not see with ordinary eyes.* You *let things come and abide in your heart and let your heart return and abide in things.*

Remembering We Have Choice

In sacred space, we have choice. Cooking is a choice we may make. Eating out is another, along with microwave, take-out, table, couch. Some homes are without a cutting board and have only a dull paring knife for prepping. Pots may be scarred and pitted. Counters cluttered. Dishwashers full—are the contents washed or unwashed? Sinks precariously piled with plates and bowls, glasses, silverware, and discarded food. Pots with the debris of unserved food sit soaking for easy cleaning, which rarely occurs, as it's not that easy to put hands to work. Other kitchens are pristine because no one ever goes there.

We make choices. About what is worth caring for and tending to. Is the food? The space? The dishes? Are you? At times no cleaning utensils are to be found: no sponges, no brushes, no bristles. A choice to be elsewhere, where it's more pleasant. And where everything is done for you.

My daughter once rented a room in a house where even the packaging for the pizzas, which had been oven-baked, was strewn about. A choice to walk away. Stoves with only one burner that works—the landlord's not fixing it—or the utilities have been turned off and no burners are available. Off-putting aromas from the refrigerator. I've been in these kitchens. There's work to be done before even beginning to cook.

Another kitchen where layers of dust and grease have turned the counters black. You don't wash it clean but scrape it like old paint, literally chiseling up curls of accumulated grime. I've found an ammonia-based cleaner applied with elbow grease and the green abrasive side of the sponge work best for removing the remaining residue—one sponge after another, as they become unusable.

Years of walking away. Years of doing the least possible to eat and be done. It's a choice. I will cook, eat, and walk away. I will not notice the grime. I will ignore what I've left behind. I am free. I do what I like. This is America. This is our world, where choice often moves in the direction of what appears to be easy and neglects the sacrifice necessary to bring forth the sacred.

The sacred is the world of spirit, the realm of the heart, which cannot be measured, bought, or sold. You offer what you have to offer because you *choose* to do so, not in order to gain accolades or accumulate people's gratitude or praise.

Our choosing may be conscious or unconscious, thoughtful or thoughtless, habitual or considered. We come by our style of choosing honestly, given our childhood experiences—that is, the unique template or model we received for how to function in this world. As we mature, we may come to realize that we could make new choices—that is, we have freedom, if we choose it!

And some of you—bless you—some of you are choosing to cook, to clean, to provide, to nourish. Sacred space doesn't come or go. It's been here all along, but when you do not practice the way of sacred space, you do not realize it. You do not know it. You can choose to be held in blessedness and spread blessedness with your efforts. You can work to acknowledge what matters.

On one hand, this is simply practical—how will you manage to have food available for placing in your mouth? On the other hand, you could be choosing to practice living in sacred space—that is, to make sacred the space you live in, the space where you are, where there is inherent worth beyond ordinary performance-based, bottom-line thinking.

Worth comes from your intention, your effort, your attention to manifesting it. In other words, along with the world's usual evaluations, your sincerity, wholeheartedness, generosity, compassion, love, care, and careful observation are also at work. When they're not at work, the sacred does not appear to be manifesting. Work then—in addition to accomplishment in worldly terms—is another word for actualizing what is innermost. And that can be challenging at times—for all of us. In worldly terms, you are not always compensated, and at times you are criticized. You actualize what is innermost because you choose to do so, not because it pays.

Freedom Beyond Rote and Chore

In our ordinary world, we learn to play by the rules, to follow the recipe, to get it right, while in sacred space, cooking (and life) can be more than just following recipes. Zen Master Tenkei advised, "See with your eyes, smell with your nose, taste with your tongue . . . nothing in the universe is hidden. What else would you have me say?" Beyond rote and chore—doing what you've been told—is the freedom to realize the way to cook, letting the ingredients come forward to awaken and nourish, letting yourself come alive to cook, to do something that you've never done before!

In our everyday world, food is fuel for the human machine—what's the best, the cheapest, least stressful way to gas up?—while in the realm of the sacred, food is mystery, source, and sustenance. Cooking is meeting the heart of the matter in meeting the ingredients, oneself, and others. Presence meeting presence.

If you want some fabulous recipes, go get a fabulous cookbook. Many are superb. *No Recipe* offers teachings about how to structure your awareness to live in sacred space and includes the cultivation of wholesome kitchen practices, such as washing and wringing out sponges (so that they are useful and do not stink!). It offers teachings about giving your attention to the food and how you can usefully interact with it.

2

YOU'RE THE COOK

Making your love manifest, transforming your spirit, good
heart, and able hands into food is a great undertaking,
one that will nourish you in the doing, in the offering, in
the eating. No one but you can do this: turning what is
invisible inside into fragrant aromas and nourishing flavors.
Books and classes will teach you to follow instructions
so that you can learn some basics and possibly reproduce
someone else's masterpieces. Coming to your senses and
knowing for yourself what's what is your task, an ongoing
journey that will have its crests and valleys, its successes
and fiascoes, as well as the sweetest fulfillment—food at
the table with warmhearted companions.

You're the Cook

You're the cook.

SUZUKI ROSHI

When I initially assumed my position as head cook (tenzo) at the fledgling Tassajara Zen Mountain Center in May of 1967, my new coworkers informed me that "we do not use salt here." Really? "Yes," they proclaimed all-knowingly, "salt is bad for you." I was at a loss what to do. To avoid conflict, should I accede to their understanding that salt is bad for you, even though no evidence was presented, or use salt and weather the consequences? I called on a higher authority and went to see Suzuki Roshi in his cabin at Tassajara.

"You're the cook," Roshi clarified in his soft yet decisive manner. "You can use salt if you want." What a relief: it would be okay to cook.

So many beliefs, so many understandings come and go, hold sway, enthrall and captivate, lose momentum. Salt is bad for you, yet macrobiotics believe in eating lots of salt, miso, and soy sauce. Some people trumpet eating only raw vegetables and fruits; others say only cooked vegetables. There are meat-eaters, vegetarians, not just vegetarian but vegans, fat phobic, fat appreciative, allergic, sensitive, intolerant, dairy approving, no dairy allowed, spicy, and plain. And this is not even mentioning comfort food versus the latest fad—excuse me, *haute* cuisine, where food is *architectural*, turned into *froths*, or goes *molecular*. Not to mention assembly by *elves* under a magnifying glass. Or maybe that's over now. All well and good—I love that people devote themselves to their craft, though I choose not to keep up with what they are doing or with the prices they charge.

When you are home in your kitchen, *you're the cook*, so you decide. Perhaps you feel confident, or possibly you sense a minefield of preferences and standards, science and circus, claims and counterclaims. Perhaps the voices argue back and forth in your head, as though in a courtroom battle: judge, jury, prosecutor, defense attorney, witnesses. The trial proceeds without end. Appeals are mounted. New evidence presented, and still you're the cook. Some people will like what you cook; other people won't. When you try to please everyone, you will still displease many.

When people come to my cooking classes, I ask them to please try out practicing cutting skills and other techniques that I share. I ask them to taste carefully, ingredient by ingredient, and let me decide how to season the various dishes we prepare. And then I remind them, "When you get home, remember that you're the cook, and you decide how to do things, which ingredients to prepare, and how to season the food."

When I was first cooking at Tassajara, I received complaints that the oatmeal was too thick: "In the morning our digestion is still sluggish and we need something easy to digest, so the oatmeal needs to be soft and liquidy and cooked a long time." Okay. Understood.

When the oatmeal was thinner (and thoroughly cooked), another group of people protested: "We're digging a septic tank by hand; we're hauling rocks. Since we're not eating meat, at least we could have oatmeal that you can chew." Okay. Got it.

Once I put raisins in the oatmeal. Yet another contingent entered the fray with angry denunciations: "Why are you poisoning everyone?" The macrobiotics were convinced that sugar was poisonous, even in the form of dried fruit, and if you followed their diet plan, you would be calm and peaceful. Raisins apparently were not in the plan. Doing your best is still not a recipe for pleasing everyone.

In Zen we say, "Follow a true teaching, while keeping your awareness open for something better, and if you find something better, then follow that." It turns out that the point is to honor your own aesthetic and to be open to having your aesthetic shift, grow, and change. Your aesthetic is something personal, yours, inside. It does not come from opinions, articles, or cookbooks. Something inside says, "Yes," and you concur, "By all means." Your work is to clarify your aesthetic—which often means seeing through your own childhood preferences—express it, trust it, and cultivate it without sticking to anything, without any evidence, without any credentials. Of course you listen to others and consider their perspective, and then, true to yourself, on you go, endlessly. Often you have something to learn. Okay, you say, "I'll try that out."

Trusting Your Aesthetic

Your aesthetic is something alive—sometimes said to be formed at conception, in utero, birth, or childhood—organically shaped first by your early life experiences and then informed and reformed by new experiences that you receive openly with interest and curiosity. You continue tasting new foods and fresh dishes. You listen to others. You entertain their views (which may often curiously be like sales pitches), but you don't have to buy in immediately. Instead, you can say, simply, "Thank you, good to know. I'll keep that in mind."

Over time many taste experiences will continue to shape your aesthetic. You learn to trust your *felt sense* because you know for yourself, not because you have the arguments ready to defend it. When you find yourself resorting to arguments, that's not an aesthetic. That's a head trip, where your mental body is busy hijacking the agenda—for better or worse.

For Zen practitioners, one's aesthetic is commonly considered to be located in the *hara*, about three finger-widths below your navel—which is loosely analogous to the second chakra. The second chakra is widely considered the seat of the felt sense. To trust your hara or felt sense, you will frequently need to disregard what everyone is saying, even what your own head is saying, as well as much of what you previously learned. Ours is a culture that believes in what the head says and that you advance in life by following the directives that come from above, from the realm of thinking. It is a culture that believes you could argue out what is right and browbeat others into following along. So learning to listen to and trust your felt sense, or your aesthetic (rather than your thinking), is a huge and important shift in awareness.

Step by step, taste by taste, you come to know that there is nothing outside this—your careful experiencing. As my Zen teacher Suzuki Roshi often repeated, pointing first to his head and then to his hara, "Zen is to settle the self on the self." As it was a verbal teaching, we never found out whether that second self below the navel had a capital *S* or a small one.

How You See Cooking

See cooking as a chore or a waste of time, and you will find the task tedious—so tiresome that you will probably not even get into the kitchen! See cooking as an opportunity to develop new skills, to learn as you go, to nourish and feed yourself, family, and friends, and your activity in the kitchen will likely flourish. Shift from your head to your heart and hands, your body and being, and you will tend to discover connection, a home ground for purifying your love, moments of meeting the Beloved, and opportunities for further renewal. What are you doing with your life? How will you choose to see things?

Cooking Is Not Just Cooking

Cooking is not just cooking.
You're working on yourself.
You're working on others.
SUZUKI ROSHI

It's not always so. It may be so, but it's not always so.
SUZUKI ROSHI

Often we characterize activities with all-embracing designations. Cooking is tiresome. Meditation is boring. Psychedelics are mind-altering. Surfing is a blast. Rock climbing is invigorating. A massage is relaxing. Sex is heavenly. Whatever we characterize with blanket descriptions, Suzuki Roshi reminded us, "It's not always so."

At least as important as the activity itself is what we implicitly bring with us when we move into action: the way we see the world and how we go about doing things. Yes, we take to some activities and not to others. Yet one most basic point of emphasis in Zen (and Buddhism) is that when we think our happiness depends on manipulating our activities to maximize the pleasurable ones and minimize those we find unpleasant, we will suffer. Because it's an inherently flawed strategy—it cannot be accomplished. The dishes remain unwashed and continue to stare back at you.

As you attempt to increase the positive moments and decrease the negative ones, you put yourself in the passive position of being powerless as experiences inflict themselves upon you. How then will you stand your ground with some strength and equanimity, digesting the various moments of your life?

The important shift here is to value the darkness as well as your capacity to develop skills to handle whatever the moment brings and to get to work—or start cooking, as it were. In other words, work means not just work in the world. You will also be working on how you see things, on what kind of effort you make, on whether or not you persevere. The activity is not in charge. You are. You have choice.

Sure, sometimes you turn to do something else. Yet other times you get to work, you work through it, you see it through, and in the process, you undergo transformation.

If cooking is "tiresome," then while you are thinking that "this cooking is tiresome," you will probably not notice any of the aspects of cooking that might be engaging, beautiful, or energizing. You will probably cook in a repetitive manner, completing assigned tasks without any sense of curiosity or discovery, without truly engaging your life-force energy, without understanding how to bring your body and spirit alive in the kitchen. In other words, cooking will be tiresome because you are doing it in a tiresome way. You're only putting in your time until you can get to somewhere your awareness can be carried along, or if all goes well, swept away. Often then, when you return to the rest of your life, it can seem even grayer—because you still have more to learn about how to meet and engage the ingredients of life.

If meditation is "boring," who said that? Who must be busy looking elsewhere for more energizing experiences rather than entering more deeply into the moment as it is? Who is not finding the way to connect what is inside with what is outside and instead is wishing for salvation or escape, whether it be in the form of the proverbial sex, drugs, and rock and roll or the allures of entertainment or enlightenment? Who is it that prefers something big and powerful to provide a sense of flight (or at least height) to coming to a standstill and having to be with oneself? And who might agree to work with this seemingly inadequate self? With careful examination, perhaps you realize that you are a great candidate for this work of re-parenting yourself, of becoming your own best friend.

Boredom can be a precursor to more intimately engaging with the present moment. Instead of busily dismissing the moment with a condescending, "Hey, meditation, you don't do it for me," you shift to, "What more can I find out? Is there something I'm missing? Tell me more." You open, or allow, for something bigger.

While you are busy being bored—that is, not finding the excitement and stimulation you are looking for—often you will not be noticing how much you are abandoning yourself in the process. While you are busy looking elsewhere, what is apparent is not yet realized. Realization is everywhere. And you? Where are you spending your time? Daydreaming about being elsewhere? Or digging in and finding *the black dragon jewel* exactly here.

Naturally we find some activities uplifting and others troublesome, but we will discover more freedom for ourselves when we do not make universal statements that leave us out of the equation. When we realize that the things we do are not just things but our *behavior*, then we may also realize we have the power to change our life by changing *the way* we do things rather than what we do.

I know that changing what we do—breaking out of unsatisfying relationships or leaving jobs that don't value our gifts—can also be an important life task, but when it's our only option, we're probably limiting our choices. Wherever you go, there you are, so finally, we're deciding if where we are is a good place to work on our problems, to develop new skills or tools, or "to have the right kind of trouble." Finding the space where you can learn and grow, entering the space where you can belong rather than just fit in means that your life can go forward. You are bringing the sacred alive.

Baking bread may seem like it's too much work, but as one of my students once shared, "Baking bread seemed like a way to reown my life from corporate America."

~

Giving Voice to What Is Inside

Connecting what is inside with what is outside, the inner world with the outer one, is the work of a lifetime, work that is often carried on deep beneath the surface of a world of surfaces.

In outer reality, where images loudly shout their self-importance and claim undue amounts of attention, where will you choose to put your attention? On crafting your image? Or working with the ingredients you're given, doing what you came here to do?

Suzuki Roshi would ask us to discover, "What is your inmost request?" Still I continue to study how to awaken ears to hear what is most intimate, to listen to the oceanic silence within. That I may follow that innermost unspoken resolve. That I may give it voice. Giving voice to our inmost request is pivotal for giving it life. Then we can make it real for all the world to see. Then the world comes forward to meet your inner vow.

Over the years, I have found one inmost request after another—and often my practice has been to work on these intentions in the kitchen:

I want to learn how to bake bread and teach others how.

I want to breathe easy.

I want to feel simply and reliably okay about being here, being at home here. Whether or not I have problems or difficulties.

I wish for intimate connection with others, with food, with the work at hand.

I long to sense what is sacred, calm, clear, and precious.

I want to stand my ground. Speak my truth.

I will learn to love myself, others, and the world the way I have always wanted to be loved.

Spiritual work in this context means giving voice to what is innermost and connecting that to the outer world. We are called to be even larger-hearted than we could possibly imagine. Loving what is less than perfect. Let's get on with it, shall we?

3

COMING TO YOUR SENSES

When you give your attention to the ingredients, you let the true spirit of the grain speak. You sense the velvety flesh of butter lettuce coming alive in your mouth, alive and then disappearing. The rigid outer world of right and wrong, good and bad, dissolves, and in complete calmness, your heart resonates buoyantly. Anytime you are still and receptive, you can meet what is from beyond. Food and cooking are an awesome place to start, and even your fiascoes are often edible, if not downright delicious. Simply take care of each moment leading to the table, giving your attention to your experience and taking action in accord with circumstances, including your own aesthetic.

Tasting the True Spirit
of the Grain

Do not arouse disdainful mind when you
prepare a broth of wild grasses; do not arouse
joyful mind when you prepare a fine cream soup.
ZEN MASTER DŌGEN

"I don't understand you Americans," Suzuki Roshi lectured us. "When you put so much milk and sugar on your cereal, how can you taste the true spirit of the grain?" How indeed? I certainly had never aspired to taste the true spirit of the grain—I had not even conceived that there was such a thing. Don't you just put on the condiments or seasonings to your liking?

In 1967 we were starting the first Zen meditation retreat community in the West, Tassajara Zen Mountain Center. Since I had been meditating for two years and had worked as a cook for all of two and a half months, I guess I was an obvious choice: Would I be willing to be head cook at the new center? Not knowing I couldn't do it, I said, "Sure."

Arriving at Tassajara in April, I learned that at breakfast we offered a wide range of condiments for the morning oatmeal, cream of wheat, or rice cream: white sugar and brown sugar certainly, and "because some people don't want to eat sugar—it's bad for you, you know," we also provided honey and molasses. Then there was milk—from cows in those days—and besides milk, we sometimes put out half and half, and for those who wanted it, canned milk. Hey, this is America—have it your way!

Roshi continued, "What? Do you think you can make every moment taste just the way you want it to? Adding milk and honey to everything?" Yes, that *is* what I'd thought. "How will you learn to appreciate the true spirit of the grain? How will you learn to experience your own true spirit? How will you learn to experience *things as they are?*"

We were receiving Buddhist teaching in a nutshell I guess, or a bowl of cereal, starting with reality being fundamentally unfixable and not tasting the way we'd like it to. Yet when we let go of fixed ideas of what we want and taste things with mindfulness and receptivity, we can come to rest or settle in the "true spirit of the grain."

Life brings a variety of flavors. Wouldn't it be liberating to simply go ahead and taste the tart or the bitter along with the sweet? The plain along with the superbly seasoned? The stress of having to doctor or fix everything can become so tedious and frustrating. And curiously enough, not being open to what is distasteful makes it all the more challenging to resonate with what is delicious. When welcomed, the oatmeal's plain, moist earthiness, hinting of sunlight, opens the heart. Tasting the heart of the oatmeal, you taste your own plain goodness. The good earth is your own good-heartedness—not fancy perhaps, but you can taste it when you let the moment come home to your heart and forget various desires to make it taste the way you want, the way it should.

To Get Started,
You Don't Need to Know

Beginner's mind is the complete original realization.
ZEN MASTER DŌGEN

Cooking, for me, has always been a sensual experience. I look, smell, taste, touch. For many of us, coming to our senses is pretty much incomprehensible. Again and again, I encounter people wanting to get it *right* and make the food according to the recipe rather than learning to trust themselves and their capacity to negotiate the way for themselves. "How much salt did you put in?" they ask, without realizing they do not know how much asparagus or tomato sauce I am putting the salt on.

I was nineteen when I began noticing that food was not arriving at the table with any regularity. Mom was twenty miles away, and it became more and more obvious that someone needed to do the cooking. I decided I would take it on. I gave myself permission to not know what I was doing—I wanted to eat! One way or another, I would figure it out. For many of us, this simple authorization to begin where we are may seem inconceivable—don't you need a lot of instruction so that you know what you are doing?

Given the challenges of kitchen work, it's no wonder that the tasks of daily life—getting to work, getting the car repaired, getting the kids to the dentist and soccer practice, paying the bills, caring for parents, friends, neighbors—keep us out of the kitchen. These days it can be even more of a dilemma with the demands of Facebook and other social media, let alone television. Coming to the decision to cook can mean profound changes in your life focus and life energy, perhaps a reordering of your priorities.

Armed with marketing hype and fortified with glossy photographs, cookbooks often seem to be selling pretense and status: recipes from the famed restaurant, or easy and stress-free recipes to impress your family and friends, or really healthy dishes to nourish your loved ones. *Does what you're cooking measure up to what we cook? Probably not. Better get our book(!) and do what we tell you.*

If you look, though, you can still find classic cookbooks that share straightforward recipes, skills, and techniques for cooking. Ones that I loved early on for instance were Julia Child's *Mastering the Art of French Cooking*, Irma Rombauer's *The Joy of Cooking*, Craig Claiborne's *The New York Times Cookbook*. When a cookbook is engaged in teaching rather than selling, you may discover a great deal of inspiration from it. See what speaks to you, and start there. And of course there are many useful newer cookbooks in addition to the ones I started with.

Ironically, I began cooking from a friend's copy of a zen macrobiotic cookbook by George Ohsawa. As macrobiotics has little or nothing to do with Zen, the designation is precisely one of those marketing ploys designed to sell: get this book because it's Zen! Though the recipes were not particularly special, it was a place to start, and most of what I was doing wasn't in the cookbook anyway: cutting the celery stalks into commas, boomerangs, and lengthy diagonal strips; marveling at the intricate cross-section of cabbage so reminiscent of trees; and playing with colors. With both a stack of small wooden bowls and a set of enamel-coated thrift-store aluminum bowls, I would try putting the carrot pieces in the wooden bowl, the magenta bowl, the emerald bowl, the silver bowl, only to shift later, perhaps as the ingredients accumulated. *Gosh, let's change that.*

Green peppers in the candy-apple cherry bowl; red peppers in the lavender. No one else would see this magnificent display of colors arrayed before cooking (should I have been a painter?), but I was finding connection with the world through food.

Almost immediately I discovered that I could cook vegetables that were delicious—that is, leaving the broccoli, the asparagus, the cabbage slightly crunchy, rather than cooking them to death. Years later, when I assisted Deborah Madison in writing *The Greens Cookbook*, we advised readers to "cook the vegetables until they are as tender as you like." Still, our copy editor asked, "How long? How do we know?" You trust your taste, until it changes, and then trust your taste. You're the cook!

Cooking wasn't just about getting something done or getting something right. I was absorbed in a world of beauty, fragrance, delight.

And I wasn't alone any longer. I had all these colorful, flavorful companions right before my eyes, speaking to me from far away. I'm remembering the white onions, orange carrots, pale green celery, and deep green bell peppers. For dinner parties, I would buy a large bottle of sake (1.5 liters, which was three dollars in those days) and busy myself serving food and refilling the little sake cups. I didn't need to be brilliantly social after all. I could provide a table and chairs. I could offer sustenance. I could provide convivial space. Smiles, bright eyes, and flowing conversation brought life and conviviality to my kitchen.

Looking back, I was beginning a lifelong love affair. Over many years, I found that if I could relate with food with warmhearted compassion, eventually I could learn to treat people with love and respect, and I could touch my own wounds with tenderness. Marriage, divorce, the passing of my Zen teachers—through it all, food and cooking have sustained me.

Permission Granted

Real freedom is to not feel limited when wearing this Zen robe,
this troublesome formal robe. Similarly, in our busy life, we should
wear this civilization without being bothered by it, without
ignoring it, without being caught by it. Without going anywhere,
without escaping it, we can find composure in this busy life.

SUZUKI ROSHI

None of this is so complicated really, yet most of us need permission: "See with your eyes, smell with your nose, taste with your tongue. Nothing in the universe is hidden. What else would you have me say?" The words of Zen Master Tenkei resonate over the centuries, and still we demand of him: "Tell me how to get it right, so nobody complains. How do I make things taste the way I like?" And the venerable one answers, "There's not enough milk and honey in the entire universe," or "Upside-down idea—what are you thinking?"

That nothing is hidden includes the impossibility of doing what you're asking, pleasing yourself and others always and everywhere. It means, as another Zen master of old said, "The secret is in you."

You could simply have your own life, come to your senses, and experience for yourself what's what. One day tasting lentil soup, I found that it didn't taste the way I wanted it to taste. Did it need more salt, pepper, lemon, garlic, oil, butter? On the other hand, why not give it a rest—is there something sacred about the flavor I have in mind that I have to make my lentils or vegetables taste *that* way? One problem with recipes is that they blind us to the reality that nothing is fixed and that we are creating reality from scratch as we go along. Beyond the recipe, could we aim to bring out the best in the food—and in one another, rather than aiming to behave properly?

Once I came across a small article in *Prevention* magazine that said a study showed food prepared well and in an aesthetically pleasing manner was more nourishing than the same ingredients prepared without care. I've always thought so, but to care about such matters is rare in our culture. Many of us give ourselves very little permission to have taste. To have taste smacks of elitism or of being picky. "Just eat it, honey; it's good for you." Or as one friend mentioned when she was being choosy, her mother would tease her, "Look who thinks she's worth sliced fruit!"

Another habit is to eat commercial product that is manufactured to grab your attention with sweetness or with salt, along with grease and perhaps a spot of salsa. Taste? Yes, enough to know that it captures my attention. Now it's time to shut down and go on automatic.

Permission to have taste is also permission to cultivate or develop taste. What do lentils taste like? How does salt change their flavor? Or pepper? Does garlic bring out the flavor of lentils or mask it? Which is which? Are we hiding the true spirit or inviting it to come forward?

You train your palate. And I believe this is a healthy way of living. It is intelligence at work, rather than blindly obeying the master—whether science, God, religion, nature, Zen, the Tao, a cookbook. *You* come alive in the process.

Studying Chinese medicine helped me to understand this. In the theory of five elements (or five phases), each flavor element has its place or purpose. Sweet flavor supports digestion, primarily in the form of complex carbohydrates. Too little sweetness or too much—refined sugars will do nicely to provide an excess—undermines digestion. (Too little or too much exercise also undermines digestion.) Similarly the sour, or tart, flavor in appropriate amounts supports the liver, while salt supports the kidneys, the bitter flavor supports the heart, and pungent elements support the lungs. Always in balance, or we could say, in aesthetically pleasing amounts and combinations.

Colors, flavors, smells—wouldn't it be much more satisfying and engaging to live in this sacred space unfolding with our compassionate attention rather than the world of rules to be followed or disobeyed? That world of rules is where we perpetually wobble on the "goodness" scale, usually resting on "not quite good enough." Ah! to taste and enjoy, to play and discover. In that world, the true nature of things comes home to your heart. All beings rejoice. Each one is best.

~~~~~~

Follow Your Nose

Take up a blade of grass and construct a treasure king's land;
enter into a particle of dust and turn the great dharma wheel.
ZEN MASTER DŌGEN

Enlightened by the ingredients, you follow your nose.

When we are captivated by the everyday, we often look for the recipe: How shall I cook so that the food comes out the way it should, no one criticizes my efforts, and I do not risk being seen as less than masterful? Heaven forbid any failure! Crafting your image, developing your brand, that's life—isn't it? Or is there more to life than looking good?

Playing it safe means cooking the same old dishes rather than chancing the expression of your taste and your understanding. Aiming to make things taste the way they should is safer than the risk of letting the ingredients speak for themselves. Yet opening to this moment, which has never happened before, we could be investigating *what is it that thus comes*. And we could be dreaming up what to make of it.

Our usual approach is to start by dreaming up a picture—that is, coming up with a recipe—of how we want things to turn out. Then we work to come up with the ingredients—the foods, the time, the energy—possibly struggling to get them all together. Then we effort to make our dream come true. It's often more work than we imagined, and the results can fail to measure up. We call this freedom—to chase after dreams. Chasing after dreams in this horizontal world most often feels vaguely unsatisfying.

We shift to bringing forth what is sacred—receiving and opening the gifts from Beyond—by first taking an inventory of the ingredients we have on hand. Next, we dream up what to do with them! With the time and energy we have available. And as we continue cooking, we continue to dream up our response to the food, to the circumstances. We are not attached to our original recipe, our original dream, trying, often forcefully, to make it come true. We are using what's on hand and dreaming up what to do next with the resources, both inner and outer, that we have available.

We wake up, come to our senses, knowing for ourself what is what—knowing what is what so profoundly that the world of ingredients reveals its secrets: explicitly the sweet or sour, the salty, the pungent, the bitter, while implicitly calm and luminous. As the ingredients begin to share their blessing, we go beyond uninspired cuisine.

Working to bring food to the table, we are working to transform ourselves from being a bystander to being the star, the center of our own life—transforming our challenges and difficulties and our afflictive emotions into nourishment. The way to do this is by doing it.

We work through it.

When you stay with the picture in your head, looking for what fits with your recipe, you may miss the quieter ingredients that are right on hand. When you are open and curious, you taste the lettuce, savor the bread, make discoveries, and find out what pleases you deeply. You're beginning to cook with feeling, to live with feeling. You mean it, putting your heart into it. You have some successes and some fiascoes. You do your best—and now it's time to do something else.

Round Apple, Smooth Banana, a Poem by Rilke

Sonnets to Orpheus: Book I, Number 13

Perfect apple, pear, and banana,
Gooseberry . . . All of these speak
death and life into the mouth . . . I sense . . .
Read it in the face of a child

who is tasting them. This comes from far away.
Are names slowly disappearing in your mouth?
In place of words, discoveries are flowing out
of the flesh of the fruit, astonished to be free.

Dare to say what it is we call "apple."
This sweetness, compressed at first,
then, gently unfolded in your tasting

Becomes clear, awake, and transparent,
double-meaninged, sunny, earthy, here—:
Oh realizing, touching, joy—immense!

RAINER MARIA RILKE, TRANSLATION BY HERMANN CLASEN AND ED BROWN

Gifts from Beyond

Many years ago, in the early '80s, when Thich Nhat Hanh was giving a talk prior to departing from the San Francisco Zen Center where I was living, he said he had a goodbye present for us. We could, he said, open and use it anytime, and if we did not find it useful, we could simply set it aside. Then he proceeded to explain that, "As you inhale, let your heart fill with compassion, and as you exhale, pour the compassion over your head."

Thich Nhat Hanh is generous with his teachings, as well as gracious and kind, and he reminded us that if we didn't know what compassion felt like or how to let it fill our chests, we could allow some warmth or light, some ease or buoyancy to fill our hearts. Pouring it over our heads, he said, could be quite relaxing and invigorating. He also mentioned that in Vietnam in the heat of the jungle they would sometimes refresh themselves using a half coconut shell attached to a handle to scoop up cool water and—here he gestured—pour it over the head. Then you let the fresh and soothing quality of the water seep down or wash through you.

It was a gift I used daily, repeatedly, for two or three years. Rough edges softened. Tension melted. Energy flowed. I had been given, I was giving myself, a renewed body, which felt more and more like home, warm and hospitable. Would you like one too? Gifts like this take practice, the practice of giving your attention, your warmheartedness to your activity.

This kind of giving, the giving of inner resources, can be done each moment under various circumstances, and we can cultivate or develop our capacity to do so while speaking with a friend, meeting a stranger, playing with our children, cooking food, washing laundry, soothing ourselves. Is there some way for it to be a gift all the way around?

The capacity to give is the capacity to receive. Often we don't know how to receive, to notice and appreciate the gifts that are ours always. Hands, for one, are ready to be hands, to massage shoulders or to shovel the dark earth. They are gifts waiting to be given, waiting to be opened, yet here we are, sitting at computers or watching television, and when it comes to cooking, we say, "Let the machines do it. I don't have time." We've forgotten the gift of our hands, the capacity to touch, handle, feel, sense; to wash, cut, cook, stir. Why bother, we wonder. It may be that we don't have time, yet we may also lack heart.

It's not the body that's weak, and it's not the hands that are unwilling. Assessing whether cooking is worth the effort is what the mind does best, and making that calculation, the mind ignores what the heart is offering: to receive the gift and pass it on. Bread cannot live by words alone. Giving and receiving go hand in hand. Given water, salt, yeast, and flour; given hands and our faithful warmhearted attention; bread appears. We let go of the heady evaluations and instead give our attention to stirring, mixing, kneading, to observing and sensing. Dough comes into being, develops elasticity, responds to the gestures we offer.

Afterward the hands tingle with vibrancy, alive and well, tension melted. We're remembering what the Shakers told one another, "Work is a gift to the person working." The person working is the first recipient of the gift of giving. By giving ourselves to the work, we receive the blessing of being alive in the present moment of eternity. We find ourselves in connection. We find ourselves at home—in sacred space.

Later still, after rising, the dough is shaped into loaves and swells up larger, and we can feel our joy swelling up as well. Warm from the oven, the bread awakens a vivid excitement and anticipation. Wonderful—an aroma close to intoxicating! The taste of earth made palatable. We belong here on earth. Can you feel it? What a gift.

The gift unopened remains inert, loses its power to invigorate and nourish. We look around for entertainment. The gift unused does not get shared and passed on. We eat out of packages that promise, "I'm quick. I'm easy. You won't have to relate to me at all. Put me in the microwave, and I'll be there for you." No wonder we grow overweight and lazy. It's too much work to actually cook.

The awesome, often unrecognized, gifts come from what is Beyond, beyond our understanding and comprehension, beyond our capacity to produce. Without our thinking, the world appears. Food comes from the bounty of nature, the work of many people, the offering of other forms of life. We cannot fathom or manufacture the lusciousness of a tomato vine-ripened in the sunlight. What is Beyond has many names: God, Emptiness, Source, the Way. It's where the Muses hang out. Even in sports we recognize what is Beyond. When a basketball player is "in the zone" and can't miss, he is said to be "unconscious."

Our eyes give us the purple of cabbage and eggplant, the red of bell peppers and strawberries, ample curves and cosmic spirals. The toastiness of summery dried grasses in roasted almonds and the mellow pungency of sautéed onions are gifts from the nose as well as nature. The mouth flows with moisture as it senses sweet, sour, salty, bitter, peppery, the flavors of earth, water, air, and sunlight. The gift is there to be acknowledged and received. Come to your senses! You could savor and delight.

Even the thoughts and ideas, the joys and sorrows, the inspirations and guesses, the play of the mind, are gifts, which could probably use a bit of cooking to make them tasteful and delicious: *Sort through and remove all loose ends, compost the soft and rotten spots, salt, season, and simmer until ready.*

The Benedictine monk Brother David Steindl-Rast told us in a lecture that "every moment of experience is a gift from God, but for it to be a gift from God, you have to receive it as a gift from God. Not to receive this moment of experience as a gift from God is what we mean by sin." An astonishing statement, as most of us had never heard it expressed this way previously! When we sit down to eat, we give thanks for this food. At the same time, we could be giving thanks for the opportunity to cook—a gift to the chef! A gift from the chef! And the gift of conviviality, the chance to share all this blessedness with one another, to share food at table in good company. Ah! Thank you eyes, ears, nose, tongue, and taste. Thank you, heart, for receiving and passing on the life-force, and thank you, hands, for taking things in hand and offering your handiwork to others.

What is it we really want? What more could we ask for than the capacity, the heart's capacity, to sense what is truly precious, to acknowledge and receive the gifts born of our care and attention, to nourish and be nourished? Hearts awaken.

What is it we really want? To be at home in this world, to be at home in this body and mind, receiving the gifts from Beyond and passing them on. The gift in working becomes the gift in eating. What more could we ask for than to activate our capacity, our heart's capacity, to sense what is truly precious, to acknowledge and receive the gifts born of our care and attention, to nourish and be nourished? No longer holding ourselves back (while we check to see if we are doing it right), hearts awaken, and we feast.

Food tastes better when the cook is joyful.

4

BRINGING SPIRIT TO LIFE

While *spiritual* is often seen as being somewhere *higher*, I am a great believer in bringing what is spiritual down to earth, making it edible, here, now. If what is spiritual is not coming down to earth, then it is up in the air, pie in the sky. I prefer my pie on a plate, at the table, with a fork handy. Spiritual for me means making the "as above, so below."

And I'm willing to see that it gets here, focusing my energy to see that it happens. Rather than a list of dos and don'ts, I prefer a direct spiritual connection without intermediaries. No small thing.

In the material or horizontal world, which we can measure and assess, we strive for a good performance, outstanding reviews, excellent grades. Are you one of the best? In the vertical world of manifesting your good heart, there is offering what you have to offer, making your best effort. And you cannot control how others will experience your offerings, so you risk their disapproval. Still, you know that you made a sincere, wholehearted effort.

Here are some stories. See what you think.

What Gets Us into the Kitchen?

I am here. I am right here. This kind of confidence is important. When you have this kind of confidence in yourself, in your being, you can practice true zazen (meditation) beyond perfect or imperfect, good or bad.
SUZUKI ROSHI

People have various motivations that come into play in the kitchen. We're each finding our own way—and some of us may get there infrequently, if at all. Years ago when I was studying Chinese medicine, I attended a workshop led by my mentors Efrem Korngold and Harriet Beinfield. To help us understand the Five Phases, including the notion that people of each type, or phase, have different fundamental approaches to life, two of us at a time sat in front of the group responding to questions. Efrem and Harriet picked each pair to represent a type.

When it was my turn, the question arose, "What's important to you in cooking?" Without thinking, I blurted out, "A sharp knife, and don't mess up my space." Hearing my response, I realized that sure enough, regretfully, I was a *metal* type. I say regretfully, because I wanted to be a *fire* type. The metal people seemed pompous and arrogant, rather know-it-all or full of it. The fire people were bright and passionate. Yet what could be more metal than wanting a sharp knife? And metal people love order: I wanted it in my kitchen.

When I share this with people who know me, they say, "But, Ed, your house is a mess. What do you mean you like order?" They have a point there—sometimes the type manifests as its opposite—but still, I love order, especially in my kitchen where everything has its place and goes back there after it is used. My kitchen would not be described as neat, but it is orderly.

Largely, I do not have to disentangle the object I wish to use. The large bowl I want is not piled underneath three, five, or eight other smaller bowls. The pans that I use regularly are hanging on hooks for easy immediate access—I just reach up and take one down—rather than piled in a drawer or a cupboard. A drawer may keep them out of sight in kitchens neater than mine, but it means opening the drawer, bending over, and sorting out the needed pan from others in the pile.

Zen Master Dōgen's teaching is in this vein: "Put what is suited to a high place in a high place, and what belongs in a low place in a low place. Those things that are in a high place will be settled there; those that are suited to be in a low place will be settled there."

Of course, I found it interesting and instructive to discover what other types said about their focus in cooking. Aside from metal, the five phases, or types, include earth, fire, wood, and water. When it was his turn, an *earth* man, friendly and large-bodied, spoke with obvious enthusiasm, saying that he loved to feed people. How simple and direct! How good is that? And down to earth! Feed people. That makes sense, I thought: provide food for others. I enjoy doing this as well, but it's not primary for me the way it was for him. "I love to anticipate people's needs and respond to them, sometimes even before they themselves realize what they want."

This man taught creative thinking at the University of California Berkeley and remarked that for him the secret was making sure that people feel safe, that they would not be attacked for what they thought. As they become confident of their safety, he noted, people's thinking becomes more creative.

A woman we identified as *wood*—willowy and graceful, with enough command to pull it off—said that her joy in cooking was organizing dinner parties and other social occasions. "I like to have all the details accounted for, to have plans in place so that the event flows smoothly and elegantly, so that I can nod my head, raise my eyebrows, or make the slightest hand gesture to indicate what needs to happen next—and it happens."

Wow! As a chef I could appreciate her devotion to doing that, and yet for myself, I don't sense sufficient implicit authority to carry it off. Others do not seem to obey me like that. Or perhaps my plan is not detailed enough. It's not that central for me. I do enough planning to get by and then let things unfold in their sometimes unruly fashion. "How dare they?" I wonder, as I notice events transpiring beyond my capacity to instruct them in required behavior.

An animated *fire* woman was asked what she found engaging about cooking. Quiet on the surface, she flashed up brightly: "The colors! The flavors! The textures! What a creative process dreaming up what to do, trying things out, experiencing what's exciting and stimulating." No argument with that. Completely brilliant: see, smell, taste, touch, experience, bring together! Just listening to her, I found myself animated. And I find this aspect of cooking high on my list as well, wanting to connect passionately with others through food, to craft the sensuality of the world into a meal.

A *water* man was the final type to share what engaged him about food. He explained that food was pivotal for him, as he owned a Chinese restaurant. What fascinated him was to study and know where a recipe came from. Which century and what part of China? Which ingredients were used at what time? How did customs change? And clearly he was a repository of considerable knowledge and operated at least one beautiful and successful restaurant.

In a similar way, people may study which foods have what constituents and figure out, at least to their own satisfaction, a plan based on their study. Where I am interested in what I can know through my experience, the water type is more drawn to what can be known through study. *Not for me*, I thought; *I want to be in the kitchen rather than the library.* Yes, I want know-how. Recipes and techniques are indispensable, but I love to be doing, to be putting the instructions into action.

At classes I have asked students to share what appeals to them about cooking, and these five responses above are some of the most common. People also mention enjoying the process, the cleaning and cutting, the stirring and baking, the stir-frying and assembly. They find pleasure in putting together ingredients for a meal, as well as delight in the magic of dishes appearing out of nowhere. Participating in this process brings them great satisfaction. Others confide that cooking is a labor of love, a place where they can give their heart to what they are doing.

And eventually I ask the room what is essential to all of this, and I answer my own question: "Actually doing it, actually being in the kitchen working. Giving your time, your attention, your hands; giving up other activities. Choosing to cook, and doing it. Without the work, without being in the kitchen laboring, the rest is idle talk, or quite possibly entertainment."

What we are learning in the kitchen is how to do it our way. If we are lucky, we are learning how to learn, studying how to study. Trying out recipes and styles of cooking, we find out something about who we are and what we have to offer.

Visiting a Spiritual Center

Let the beauty we love be what we do.
There are hundreds of ways to kneel and kiss the ground.
RUMI

When my daughter was in college, we went to visit a spiritual center together. As it was more than twenty years ago, I am hoping that the statute of limitations on whatever I might say at this point has expired, and of course we do not know what the center might be like today, if it is still there.

I am not remembering the occasion for our visit, but someone was kindly showing us around. First we went into a large room, which turned out to be a potting studio. Our guide informed us that the several people working here were crafting clay pieces that would be fired and then assembled into a sixteen-foot golden Buddha. "That sounds like a lot of intricate work," I ventured to say. "Yes, but it's terribly important for us to show our veneration of the Buddha."

We went on to another spacious room, which was bright and airy. A number of people were sitting at desks or tables with good lighting, absorbed in their activity. Our guide explained that they were writing mantras on small pieces of paper and that they would be writing enough mantras to fill the sixteen-foot golden Buddha. "That will surely be a great deal of mantra writing," I suggested. "Yes, a great deal of mantra writing, but it will make the Buddha all the more sacred."

On we went to a room vibrant with golden light and full of sewing machines. Bright yellow fabric was being sewn into robes for the Lama Dances. "They're working very hard," I mentioned, "I can see that." "Absolutely. It's important because the Lama Dances are an auspicious ceremonial aspect of our practice together, a way to share blessings with all beings."

Soon we came to yet another room with an open space where people were clothed in workout attire. These people, we were informed, were practicing for the Lama Dances. "That's a pretty unique opportunity," I offered. "Yes, unique, and a vitally important spiritual practice." We watched for a while and then went on with our tour.

In a small dim room, seemingly underground, we met the cook. Compared with the other spacious, well-lit rooms we had visited, this room felt like a dungeon. I cannot remember the circumstances—whether the cook had invited me in the first place or whether we simply ran into her. Perhaps we were offered tea—and there she was, worn and weathered from her labors. "I can't get anyone to help me," she explained. "They're all busy doing spiritual practice."

"And cooking isn't seen as spiritual?"

"If it is, then I must be getting a ton of merit. Everyone has more important spiritual practices to attend to."

"You're doing real bodhisattva practice—benefiting others, being of service."

"Yes, indeed, being of service to others who do not appreciate it!"

"Your choice."

"My choice, and I don't know what to do—the work is overwhelming. I don't have any help, and I don't know that I have the heart for it."

Welcome to the world of cooking. How do you see it?

At this point, I needed a bathroom break, so the cook directed me to the restrooms.

Here by the urinals, the floor was wet, which did not seem especially important until I flushed after urinating, and water overflowed onto the floor. I could only surmise that plumbing, along with cooking, was not considered a spiritual practice. The lesser, ordinary people who were not specifically devoted to the "spiritual" would have to take care of it—if we could only find them.

Apparently, those busy accumulating spiritual merit were above and beyond both cooking and plumbing. What a waste of time that kind of work would be when you could be accumulating spiritual merit. And how valuable that was! Perhaps they could trade it in for any plumbing or cooking they might require. Though, isn't the thought of accumulating spiritual merit a rather materialistic idea?

Not that a spiritual community is different from any other community, as this understanding is fairly common in the outside world as well, which often seems to be saying, "I'm too busy to cook (or I have more important things to do). Let's leave the cooking to those less savvy about how to avoid it or to those less advantaged who must work out of necessity. Cooking would be beneath me. It would be too much work. If I want to work out, I can go to the gym or head out on my bicycle."

As we were driving away from the center, my daughter had the last word, "Dad, were those people spaced-out when they got there, or does the practice make them that way?"

"Gosh, I don't know. We're all found and lost and finding our way."

Visiting Another Spiritual Center

Some months later, I was at another spiritual center where a visiting teacher was extolling the virtues of meditation, saying that the meditation hall was the most auspicious place to acquire spiritual merit. As he spoke about this at some length, I began to wonder who would be doing the cooking, so when it came time for questions, I approached the microphone: "You've said that the meditation hall is the most auspicious place to do spiritual practice, yet somebody needs to do the cooking and the plumbing. Is there any hope for those working outside the meditation hall, or are they relegated to a less advanced spiritual life than those fortunate enough to be in the meditation hall?"

When the visiting teacher began by saying that the meditation hall truly was the most auspicious place to practice, my heart sank. But then he continued to say that "when you give yourself to an activity and do it with complete wholeheartedness, it is *exactly* the same thing." *If only you would mention this a bit more often*, I found myself thinking, *then the cooks and plumbers would receive much more support and help.*

When you get down to it, where finally is the place to put your effort, to give your heart willingly? Where indeed? If those in the meditation hall are above working with food and plumbing, the basics of human life, how auspicious could that be? Giving yourself completely to what you are doing is precious, in the meditation hall and in the kitchen. The difference is that nobody is going to be eating your cushion time, whether your cushion time is spent facing the wall of the meditation hall or the television screen.

Offering a slice of homemade bread, born of your time and effort, hearts rejoice.

5

THE WORK OF
BEING EMBODIED

Since many of us have never studied how to do this work
of being embodied and relating with onions, cabbages, and
potatoes, the prospect of digging in and persevering can
be daunting. Often we are more accustomed to letting our
awareness go to one of its more habitual haunts, which does
not require physically putting our body (or imagined self)
on the line. When you are unaccustomed to work, it may
feel awkward and unfamiliar. You may find yourself in places
where you do not know what to do. Initially, your reaction to
being lost may be a wish to seek the familiar: *Get me out of here*,
complains the voice inside. *Get me out of here and back to what
is familiar, where I know what I am doing and can be successful
at it.* Working in this unfamiliar place of not knowing rather
than seeking a comfortable refuge is what marks the hero's
journey—your willingness to undertake rigorous adventure
and in the process undergo transformation. Work also
means handling innumerable moments of the same old stuff.
Surprisingly, as you focus on finding your way (one celery stick
at a time), you begin finding ease on the spot.

The Energetics of Zen Work

When you wash rice and prepare vegetables, you must do it with
your own hands and with your own eyes, making sincere effort.
Do not be idle even for a moment. Do not be careful about
one thing and careless about another. Do not give away your
opportunity even if it is merely a drop in the ocean of merit.
Do not fail to place even a single particle of earth at the
summit of the mountain of wholesome deeds.

ZEN MASTER DŌGEN

The Zen tradition of work is called *soji*. Much of it involves cleaning: the floors, the walkways, the toilets. When I was a practicing student of Zen back in the 1960s and 1970s, we Westerners—sometimes hippy and long-haired—would challenge our Japanese Zen teachers: "What's so spiritual about *clean*?" Or as one koan puts it, "How can you clean what has never been soiled?"

Our mentors were quite patient with us, trying again and again to explain that it wasn't that clean was more spiritual than dirty, but that we were practicing relating with things—touching them, tending to them, being in connection with them, not taking them for granted. When you practice this, you are living in another world, a world where things embody your spirit, where your presence gives things presence. We hardly have language for this: Things are simply things, aren't they? Yet when you practice caring for, tending to things, things are not just things. They are an embodiment of your spirit.

They are an embodiment of Source. To clean with this spirit or understanding is to tend the Sacred Body, to live in Sacred Space.

So we clean to create and develop a relationship between the one cleaning and that which is being cleaned. Often the object of our efforts is already clean—for example, the floor of the meditation hall. Although it is already clean, I clean it. Now in relationship, I know the floor in my body, in my knees and my hands, and I can ask the floor to ground the room and everyone practicing. I am held, supported, and I am touched, as I have touched the floor.

It is very similar to *reincarnating* into your own body: "I live here." Thus, to clean is to *reincarnate* into the world by touching it, in this case with a damp towel. Body to body we meet and smile a slight smile. "Welcome home," we say to each other. "Nice to see you again." The more closely we relate with food, pots, pans, bowls, utensils, sponges, mops, the more they reincarnate with us. Mystery of mysteries—the power we have is the power to pick up a broom. Gathering wood and carrying water, we make ourselves at home here on planet Earth—"supernatural power and marvelous activity" is the age-old Zen expression for this wood-and-water activity.

Curiously, I hesitate to write about soji because I do not want to lecture or sound like I am giving out directives. Everyone has choice about what to do with their time here on earth and how to do it. Work seems to be an area where we assume we do not have choice. There are things you have to do, and when you get done doing them, then you can spend time doing what you enjoy. In his down-to-earth book *What Are People For?* Wendell Berry wrote about the pleasure of work. "What fun," his granddaughter remarks after a day of labor—but as a culture, the sense of energetically manifesting work seems sadly lacking. Pleasure is lying on the beach or surfing the net, not using your hands to connect with the world. Yet without connecting to your body and the world, the sense of home, ease, and contentment is often absent. We create it by living it, or we may wander.

In Zen we say: "Throw yourself into the activity. Burn yourself completely." It's a practice that some of us choose, a generosity of spirit, an abundance of hands, finding out what to do, how to do it. Discovering how to give life to life, a life of the spirit manifesting in the material world, the inner coming to the surface and connecting with what is outer.

I've spent much of my life studying how to work, especially in kitchens—the dishes, the pots and pans, the floors, the compost; being a busboy, a waiter, a dishwasher. And when I say studying, much of it involves how to give myself to the activity rather than begrudging my time and my attention, letting my heart return and abide in things, simply giving myself. Sometimes it seems so old-fashioned, so embarrassing—menial labor, which implies humble, unskilled, low status, inferior, degrading—yet repetitive, warmhearted efforts often create convivial space, home.

I am trying, of course, not to make this a matter of good and bad, right and wrong, as there are homes with objects strewn about that feel friendly, and similarly, immaculate spaces that feel claustrophobic. The feeling is in the air.

As a claim to fame or recognition, physical labor does not especially qualify. When I write up my bio for leading a retreat, I mention the books that I've written rather than saying that I clean up after myself in the kitchen. So, being sincere and hardworking at menial labor is not something I do for acclaim but an activity that brings the world alive, as well as invigorating me in the process. And frankly, I've never found I could eat acclaim the way I can feast on a breakfast omelet.

When I was first practicing at the Zen Center, in 1965, during work periods Katagiri Roshi would run bent over across the zendo, pushing a towel wrapped around a block of wood to polish the floor. Watching him was an inspiration. I marveled at his grace and humility, his sheer athleticism: *he's bent over running across the floor!* Back and forth, back and forth. He wasn't there to direct the work but to do it—an incarnate example of Zen practice. He put his body on the line with focus and energy, sincere and wholehearted, without complaint, without bragging. Though fifty years have passed, the image is still vivid. That was Zen! I know we've all seen photos of Zen masters sitting imperturbably, but for me, Katagiri Roshi's racing across the zendo is the picture that stands out. We don't just sit there; we make it happen. We don't stop to think about it; we get down and dirty.

If you are curious and pause to consider, you'll have occasion to look at how you view what you are doing. You'll see if your work is a way of complying to prevent criticism, if you are doing chores as though by rote, looking forward to getting off and having time for yourself, or perhaps you sense your work is an offering that you choose to share with others, as a gift you receive and pass on. You may believe that you are a maid slaving away or a bodhisattva saving inanimate beings, or you may be on the sidelines watching.

To start where you are, take responsibility for what you are doing. If you have a default approach to work, such as avoiding it when possible, please reflect whether that's your choosing. Albert Einstein, that closet Buddhist, once said, "Insanity is doing the same thing over and over and expecting different results." New choices coming from the depths of your being will bring new life.

Everybody Loves Raking

There is no need for you to be a great person. In your limited activity, you should find out the true meaning of yourself . . . If you pick up a small stone, you have the whole universe.

SUZUKI ROSHI

"Everybody loves raking as a temple activity," my friend Gil explained to me after he returned from his sojourn practicing Zen in Japan and vipassana in Southeast Asia. "In Japan they say, 'When you rake, just rake,' while in Southeast Asia they explain, 'When you rake, watch your mind.' So in Japan, the monks can be seen raking energetically, sometimes stirring up a cloud of dust, while in Southeast Asia, the monks sometimes stand unmoving with a rake in their hands."

When I shared Gil's story with our Zen Mentor Sojun Mel Weitsman, his response was, "Sounds like the monks who stand unmoving still think their minds are up here," his index finger rising to point to his head. In Zen, activity itself is also mind. Watch the moving!

Though raking is an excellent example, the story brings to mind that there is more than one approach to daily life: eating, sleeping, cooking; work, errands, perhaps a commute; partners, children; the gym, a hike. Action and reflection are each important, and we would do well to cultivate a workable balance between being energized to get things done and being attuned to tracking our awareness. Still, when it comes to working in a kitchen with an anticipated meal time, I want to see work happening—that is, I want to see bodies in motion, arms and hands tending to the details of preparation, the onions and carrots being cut, the bowls and pots being cleaned. If you want to stand still watching your mind, you can do that on your own time or in someone else's kitchen. In my kitchen, I ask for focus on the work at hand.

Sometimes, those focused on remaining calm and contained are not always learning the skills necessary to perform, to function in the world. They may be stable and not raise their voice in the kitchen, but they don't know how to make a salad dressing. They may meditate steadfastly but not develop their communication skills. While busy generating calm, beautiful states of minds, they are not developing the skills, capacities, and practices that could actually and realistically manifest delicious food or wholesome relationships.

To grow up in the real-life, how-to-do-it world cultivating explicitly useful ways to live well and harmoniously is the way of benefiting yourself and others—learning how it's done here on planet Earth. Learning to prepare food, you are also studying how to handle emotions. So my interest in addressing and encouraging a spiritual life in the kitchen includes preparing beautiful food. Let's make it happen. In this way, the more formal expression is, "Don't look for nirvana outside of samsara." You do not find the peace and serenity of the vertical world by ignoring or abandoning everyday reality. You study how to work with it. And when to rest.

As a committed Zen student doing residential practice under institutional supervision, I often practiced watching my mind. Still, I keep finding that if I am going to do something, I need intention, focus, energy, commitment, and I need to study how to prepare bean soups and vegetable soups or how to assemble a vinaigrette. Clearly I will need to connect my awareness to the things of this world so that they manifest as food. It's up to me to make it happen. I'm going to work with things, and things are going to work with me. We'll see what happens. If I don't go into the kitchen, I don't eat. Maybe things happen differently in your world.

Watching the mind tends to go along with *accepting what's offered*, which is an important practice. Monks and nuns go out on rounds begging for food—take what you get. Originally they did not stay more than three nights in one place, although an exception was made for the rainy season. Apparently this did not sit well with the Chinese when Buddhism arrived there and the Zen school developed. One of the early masters was adamant: "A day of no work is a day of no eating." Do things with your body. Don't just realize the dharma; manifest it.

Let the fundamentally unstoppable energy of the universe come through into your activity.

Of course, when we have habits of mind that use physical violence to solve things, we could use some clear, careful observation so that we learn how to ride the waves of energy, producing a fire in the hearth rather than a thunderbolt. The energy that can destroy is also the energy that can nourish. By watching the mind, by tending the mind, we can discover how to modulate our energy and refocus our efforts on harmonizing rather than overpowering. And sometimes committing ourselves to simple, straightforward tasks is ever so helpful for transforming our energy.

Conversely, watching the mind does not activate great energy. You may become calm and tranquil, still and peaceful, and you may also daydream or offer an ongoing critique on reality. If this is an old habit for you, you may become very good at it. Applying the antidotes effectively, you may quiet your mind anew—and actually rake.

Sometimes, of course, energetic devotion to an activity is valuable for cutting through, whether it is the classic practice of bowing or work in the fields or in the kitchen. You devote yourself so energetically to a physical activity that you simply do not have time, energy, or space to think. Temporarily at least, you've cut off the tentacles of thought and emotion and actualized yourself freely. Some degree of your usual preoccupations can wash through and out.

How sweet is that?

Though I have done both of these practices extensively, when I am at a loss, I come back to *do what you're doing*—cutting the carrots, stirring the soup. The interesting point here is that this is not a matter of determining what is right or wrong or deciding what is the best practice and then following the decision we have carefully weighed out. We do what is useful on the occasion, and if we've been observing, what we do accords with our personal aesthetic.

Simply put, for me pleasure arises when I use my body to do things. Naturally enough, difficulty, obstacles, and setbacks come along for the ride, and I pause in my doings to empty the compost bucket, clear the dish drainer, get out the cheese grater, wipe up the spill. Above-average baseball players get three hits for every ten at-bats; in basketball, making over half your shots is phenomenal. We miss because we make the effort. When you are not taking your shots, you are not in the game. I cook because I enjoy it. I study how to show up, be present and absorbed, without being tight or high-strung (not always hitting the mark).

6

FEELING YOUR WAY
ALONG IN THE DARK

Your willingness to do the work of relating closely with
the particulars of the moment arouses spark and vitality.
No, it's not always coming out the way you want, yet you
will find the way to work with it, all of it. Your choosing
to seek the way exactly here in this uncomfortable, often
dark place, where all seems lost or misshapen, elicits
resources you didn't know you had. As you continue
choosing to find the way to work with obstacles, you
more and more trust your capacity to respond from the
depth and breadth of your being. While cooking, you
are getting cooked, through and through. You appear to
yourself as someone you never met before: your sincerity
and wholeheartedness are a work in progress, beautiful to
behold! And the food's not bad as well.

Cooking with Passion

Zen is like feeling your way along in the dark.
SUZUKI ROSHI

*The most important point is to find out
what is the most important point.*
SUZUKI ROSHI

At a *sesshin* (meditation intensive) one year, Suzuki Roshi lectured us, "Zen is like feeling your way along in the dark," and he extended his hand out in front of him, feeling this way and that. "You might think it would be better to have more light, to know where you are going, and to get there in a hurry, but Zen is feeling your way along in the dark. When you have plenty of light and know where you are going, then you get impatient and want to push things out of your way. When you are in the dark, you become more careful and sensitive to what is happening around you."

At the *shosan* ceremony that followed sesshin, where each student asks the Roshi a question in public, I asked, "Feeling my way along in the dark, and now that sesshin is over, how about if we have a party?"

"If you do it with that spirit, it will be perfectly okay."

Wonderful, I thought and started to get up from kneeling in front of Roshi when his voice—"the most important point"—brought my movement to an abrupt stop, and I settled back down to listen.

"The most important point," and he paused, while I prompted myself to listen intently as the words slowly came out, "is . . . to find out . . . what is . . . the most important point."

And I thought he was going to tell me! Only he had. By looking for the most important point, I discovered gratitude and sincerity, generosity and perseverance. Over many months, I kept finding one thing after another: gratitude, joy, sincerity, interest, compassion. And still I continue to investigate.

One of the places where I have studied this is in the kitchen. What is the most important point? For a Buddhist, there are many ready-made answers: being mindful, being silent, watching your mind, being calm and peaceful. All well and good, but did anyone say preparing food? We would do well to study how we do what we are doing—what is the most important point?—because as Suzuki Roshi mentioned, "If I tell you something, you will stick to it, but it is not always so. When you stick to something that I say, you will abandon your capacity to study and investigate for yourself."

Buddhists proverbially note the importance of being mindful. Mindfulness practice—simply *noting* an experience without assessing good or bad, right or wrong—is probably the most essential skill and the most basic tool for cultivating deeper awareness. Unfortunately, the word, especially now, is overused and used without precision. So, for example, when people do not pick up after themselves while working, they are characterized as not being mindful. If they gossip while cooking, that's not mindful. In other words, when someone is not doing what you think they should, they are not being mindful. So to be mindful becomes to *do it right*, the way you are supposed to according to the rules. In other words, *not mindful* becomes a way of saying behavior was wrong or bad according to the speaker's assessment.

In this case, you'll continue to be caught in the realm of thinking rather than observing for yourself how things happen in your experience and using that information to possibly make better choices for yourself. When you observe closely how things happen in your experience, change comes from you, out of your experience, rather than being implemented top down from your thinking. "Don't put another head over your head," is a Zen saying. So it's best to use mindfulness as an awareness practice and not as a weapon to attack others or yourself for so-called improper behavior.

Do you want to prepare food or be a good Buddhist? Is there a way to do both? In our everyday world, there are similar questions. Do you want to solicit cooperation or defeat the other person? Do you keep quiet and mind your own business so that people will like you and not criticize what you say? Do you aim to establish positive shared intention, or do you blame others to establish your higher position? Do you mop up a spill on the floor or walk past thinking it's someone else's job? Who gets to say? Moment by moment, we can be finding out what to do by examining our inmost request.

While basic mindfulness practice in the kitchen can be useful, I will offer some alternatives as well. Still, I would encourage you to feel your way along in the dark and to investigate the most important point. In others words, find out for yourself how to make working in the kitchen a source of spiritual awakening—making yourself at home, enhancing your well-being, bringing your brightness, integrity, and wholeheartedness alive in the work.

When I asked Suzuki Roshi for his advice about working in the kitchen, he said, "When you wash the rice, wash the rice. When you cut the carrots, cut the carrots. When you stir the soup, stir the soup." Though similar, this is not the same as "be mindful in the kitchen," which may sound as though you have two things to do: washing and being mindful, cutting and being mindful, stirring and being mindful. On occasion the mindfulness part will look a bit stiff, as your impulse will be to move slowly and carefully enough that only a moderate amount of energy and emotion arises to meet the circumstances. In other words, most people hear "be mindful" as keep yourself in check, or turn the volume down on yourself. Often enough then, we do not know how to throw ourselves into the work of cooking.

What is magnificent and magical is finding out how to manifest the cutting of carrots with your whole body and mind and how to wash the rice with your eyes and your hands, connecting consciousness with the senses and the world—not just going through the motions.

This brings me to a pivotally important point. When you stop going through the motions and instead manifest the stirring of soup, alive in the present moment, emotions may surface. While some Buddhists find this problematic and seemingly recommend dispassion, my suggestion is to invite your passion to cook. Instead of tying yourself down so that nothing volatile arises, use what is vibrant and volatile—feelings—to energize your presence in the kitchen. Instead of telling your emotions to go away or acting them out with violence or volume, invite them to handle, stir, wash, touch, scrub, scour; invite them to see, smell, taste, and delight in the play. Emotions become unworkable when we do not work with them—that is, when we want them to disappear without acknowledging them.

The cook's temperament is a passion for life. Give it a field in which to practice. Put it to work. If I were to cook only when I feel loving, kind, and benevolent, I would have starved long ago. Please understand that I am not telling you to *act out* in the kitchen. My encouragement is to turn afflictive emotions, as well as enthusiasm and exuberance, into something edible and nourishing—food.

Washing the rice when you wash the rice is also putting emphasis on concentration, focus, attention, and energy. These actions rather blend together: wash, cut, cook, taste, savor. You gather yourself, as many disparate parts as you can muster, and zero in on the activity and how to do it easily, effectively, effortlessly (not just acting out of habit). Give your attention to observing and perceiving. Let your life-force bloom. Interact. You are making food real. It's not just talk—we can eat it.

Zen Master Dōgen advises, "Let things come and abide in your heart. Let your heart return and abide in things. All through the day and night." With our hearts, we can meet and connect, and out of that meeting and connecting, we respond. Responding from the heart, our implicit intention is to bring out the best. We are learning to relate with the things of this world and our own body-mind, rather than hiding out in a place where you don't have to relate with anything. (In Zen this lack of a place to hide out is called "not setting up a nest or a den.") You and the world are mutually arising, and you are not in charge. While leading, you follow, and while following, you lead.

You can master recipes to get it right and gain approval, but there are no recipes for telling you what your heart knows and precious little workable advice for trusting your heart rather than your head. You practice finding your way in the dark. Your capacity for cooking will grow and develop from your devotion to being in the dark, not knowing what to do, but carefully finding your way. Touch with your hands, see with your eyes, smell with your nose, taste with your tongue. *Let things come and abide in your heart. Let your heart return and abide in things.*

Manufactured products say: "I'm quick. I'm easy. You won't have to relate with me at all. Put me in the microwave, and I'll be there for you, just the way you want me to." Recipes say: "Do what I tell you, and everything will be okay. You too can make masterpieces (and if it's not going to be a masterpiece don't even bother)."

To engage with the world of cooking is to study what to do with a potato, a carrot, cabbages and bell peppers. More and more, your close experience of cooking encourages you to trust your own aesthetic, and the sometimes uncomfortable feedback from others and the food itself work to inform your aesthetic further. Are you in the dark yet? You become intimate with cooking through cooking.

Seeing Virtue

What you look for, you'll get more of it.
BECKY BAILEY IN *EASY TO LOVE, DIFFICULT TO DISCIPLINE*

After a number of months as the cook at Tassajara, I went to Suzuki Roshi with another problem: "How do I get my fellow workers to practice the way they should?" I explained to him that I was endeavoring to practice his instruction to *wash the rice* but that others in the kitchen often came late to work, disappeared for long bathroom breaks, and when they opened their mouths to gossip, chat, or patter, their hands stopped moving. "How do I get them to practice Zen?"

Roshi listened attentively, as his nods punctuated my litany with what I took as confirmation: *Yes, I know. It's hard to get good help these days.* He seemed so completely sympathetic. When I finished speaking, he paused for a bit and then startled me by saying: "If you want to see virtue, you'll have to have a calm mind."

That, I protested to myself, *is not what I asked you.* Then, the next moment, I relented, "I guess I have something new to study."

So many things are important in Buddhist practice: the Four Noble Truths, the Five Spiritual Faculties, the Six Paramitas, the Seven Wings of Enlightenment, the Noble Eightfold Path. How will you survive the kitchen? Making it through the fire? One key I found is not to calm my mind first and then look for virtue, but simply to *look for virtue*. There it is. "What you look for, you'll get more of it." When you look for fault, you'll find it. I started looking for virtue, and I began finding it.

Seeing virtue encompasses two aspects: the particulars and the absolute. When you taste what you put in your mouth, you may notice sweet or sour, earthy or sunny, and along with these relative characteristics you can sense something essential, *something* from Beyond. This something is *not a thing*. Go ahead and taste it—the virtue inherent in your careful, attentive, receptive experiencing of the moment. When your awareness is in the dark and you are opening your perception, you can also taste your own inherent goodness and the virtue of others working with you. You may meet sincerity, kindness, wholeheartedness, vulnerability, grief, anxiety, determination, stubbornness, and mind itself, vast and spacious. Awesome!

Shifting your effort, shifting your attention, from doing it "right" or aiming to gain approval, you shift to meeting and working with the ingredients at hand. Looking to see what is available, you dream up what to do with the ingredients while honoring their virtue. Our ordinary effort is to dream up a picture of how we want things to be and endeavor to make it come true. Now in the dark, you feel your way along, and your wisdom flashes: a salad, a soup, the virtue of spinach, apple, and walnut speaks to you.

The body comes alive because you are *doing* something. Yes, it's good to stop and sit and allow the usual impulses for motion an opportunity to move inwardly instead of outwardly—beautiful work there. Yet hands love to be hands.

You give them life by allowing them to find out how to do things, how to wash and cut, stir and knead, ladle and mop. Your consciousness comes out of its nest or den in the head and finds its way into activity. Hands have an eye in the middle of the palm that can see and connect with the object of touch. (In Buddhist iconography, this is pictured as Avalokiteśvara, the bodhisattva of compassion, having an eye in the middle of each palm—sometimes a thousand of them—that can heal all suffering and distress.) In this connection is health and healing, and in this way, you are learning to work with the virtue of things and to receive the blessings of being human.

Pause and Investigate

Everybody knows that cooking can be stressful. When your awareness is headed toward overwhelm, stop for a few moments and make a mental (or even written) checklist of what needs to be done. Revise your list in accordance with reality. How much time and energy do you have? Sort out what is the one thing to do next, so that you can give that one thing your undivided attention. Again, when stressed, stop and check, pause and investigate, before proceeding.

As Suzuki Roshi said, "When you are in the dark, you don't know where you are going, but when you carefully feel your way along, where you find yourself will be okay." To your health and happiness, joy and well-being, in the kitchen and out! Let's taste the blessings of the moment.

7

CAREFUL OBSERVATION
OF THE OBVIOUS

Tasting what you put in your mouth, you discover
cascades of flavor, with rapids and shallows, flowing
through unexplored terrain. When absorbed in the
activity of cooking, you are inviting the love from
Beyond to move through your heart and hands, through
your tongue and taste. You work to bring out the best
in the ingredients. Sharing joy, delight, and sustenance
with those you serve, you swim in absorption, free of
the urge to measure or assess your performance. You are
alive and well, well loved and loving well, with no more
worry about not being perfect. And you go from there.

Knowing the Differences
That Make a Difference

Thus, do not be careless even when you work with poor materials,
and sustain your efforts even when you have excellent materials.
Never change your attitude according to the materials.

ZEN MASTER DŌGEN

One of a cook's jobs is to notice differences and to investigate which differences make a difference to you in your cooking. In this way, a cook examines and decides which work is worth the effort. Evaluating which work is worth the effort includes understanding how much time and energy you have available, as well as how much help. A few examples. The tart flavor, especially lemon, gives food an upbeat, vibrant flavor. Is it worth tasting the broccoli and assessing if it could use some lemon? And if so, is it worth juicing a fresh lemon, or will you use bottled lemon juice?

It's not going to work to put lemon in every dish, but if you taste the broccoli (and if necessary season a small amount separately), you can decide. In my world, freshly squeezed lemon juice makes enough of a difference that I do the work to make it happen. Bottled lemon shifts the flavor, yet for me, some essential vitality is missing, and a bottled flavor is overly apparent (though at times I enjoy the food of others brightened to some degree with bottled lemon or lime juice).

In my study of mushroom cleaning, I have concluded that the mushrooms need not be delicately hand-toweled. I'm willing to study further to be convinced otherwise, but I have not been yet. Once with a group of students, we prepared three groups of mushrooms: cleaned with a damp towel, washed in water, and washed in water with white flour. Each batch was sautéed in butter with salt judiciously hand-sprinkled. We could not taste any difference, though the slices of hand-wiped mushrooms appeared to be more distinctly individual rather than blending into an indistinct mass of mushroom slices. Some cooks may choose to hand-wipe for this more pristine appearance, but it does not accord with my aesthetic of *country* cooking—and more often than not, my mushrooms are part of a stir-fry, so they appear distinct in any case. If there was a difference in the flavor, we with our perhaps uneducated palates could not taste it. Quite possibly others can, or perhaps it's more a concern with texture and appearance.

How one prepares lettuce salads is another case in point. Which differences make a difference? Nowadays some people say that you *have to* tear the lettuce. Oh really? In order to accomplish what? Would the point be for the salad to appear beautiful on the plate? How will you accomplish this?

When I started cooking fifty years ago, most of the knives were carbon steel, which reacted with the acid in the lettuce and left the cut surfaces brown. To cut lettuce, we would switch to a stainless-steel bread knife. Yet with the technology of how newer knives have been made for years now, lettuce can be cut without leaving any telltale brown edges. On the other hand, brown edges may appear when people tear lettuce, as they often take a number of leaves at once (to save time and effort) and rip them apart. To do this, it is necessary to firmly grip the leaves of lettuce so that unintentionally they become bruised in the handling. Is this more beautiful—bruised lettuce leaves? And some of the battered, torn leaves are so seriously misshapen that you don't dare try to get the piece of lettuce in your mouth without first cutting it with your knife. Not appetizing.

Romaine lettuce especially can be cut lengthwise down the ribs and then sideways into one-inch pieces: beautiful and elegant compared to the pieces torn by hand—classic for prepping Caesar salad. What I'm writing about here obviously does not apply to the delicate salads made of tender baby lettuces—these you don't cut and don't tear. The labor of other hands—picking all these small lettuces and handling them with great care, boxing them, trucking them—has done the work for you.

Studying differences, you'll be able to experience for yourself how the lettuce appears and how the lettuce tastes. Instead of following the book, try it out, cutting and tearing both, and observe for yourself which works for you. Consider the time and effort involved and the appearance of the result. I find that I often like cutting the lettuce down the central stem and then proceeding from there, sometimes tearing, sometimes cutting.

Once in Venice, at a cooking class with my dear friend Robert Reynolds, we tore fresh basil by hand for our pesto, our hands becoming black with the essence of basilicum. The pesto was heavenly, singing with joy, *You've released my soul!* If the aunts and grandmothers are helping, as they often do in Italy, perhaps they will take care of this project for you; otherwise, moderate slicing by hand into julienne strips will bring you closer than the Cuisinart. Perhaps along with some macerating with a mortar and pestle.

The Flavor of Today

*A teacher of old said: "Two-thirds of your life has passed,
not polishing even a spot of your source of sacredness.
You devour your life; your days are busy with this and that.
If you don't turn around at my shout, what can I do?"*
QUOTED BY ZEN MASTER DŌGEN IN *INSTRUCTIONS FOR THE COOK*

What about taste? How is it that food tastes the way it does? Is taste dependent on the food or on the awareness that you bring to the table? Both, of course—you are bringing the food and yourself to the table! Here are some stories.

When I teach cooking classes, I often encourage people to "taste what you put in your mouth." As we try out a soup or a sauce, a slice of fennel or apple, one common response is, "What should I be tasting?" Even before putting something into their mouths, my students often want to get it right, not realizing that when they aim to get it right, they will probably ignore most of what they are experiencing while looking for the one element of taste that might be identified as correct. In other words, looking for the right experience turns out to be an effective way to disempower yourself. Much of what you might experience disappears from view while you seek the right experience.

Curiously enough, though, there are circumstances for learning the requisite vocabulary. In one article I read about tea tasting, students are presented with twenty different teas that share the characteristic under study, whether it is "bright," "bold," or "brisk." Once you learn to recognize and catalog each aspect under consideration, you can become a tea taster.

To empower yourself, to liberate yourself in the kitchen: taste what you put in your mouth. Of course, the same is true in yoga, in your relationships, the same is true everywhere: experience what you are experiencing. It's free. It's precious. There's vitality. You'll know for yourself what you see, what you smell, what you taste. You are you, and you are the authority on what you are experiencing. And, of course, the big obstacle here is to remember that you are not the authority on what is going on with others (perhaps characterizing them as being "mean" or "insensitive" when they are merely acting in their customary fashion without regard for what your experience may be). Trying to control what others are experiencing is when we easily get confused or stressed, as it cannot be done.

Nor can we control our own experience. When I first made biscuits at Tassajara, they did not come out right. I tried making biscuits with eggs and without eggs, with shortening, with butter, with water, with milk. They still were not coming out right. Finally, one day I thought, *Right compared to what?*

Pretty quickly, I remembered growing up with Bisquick biscuits and Pillsbury biscuits. With Bisquick, I put some mix in a bowl and stirred in milk with a fork. Then, not even rolling it out, I simply *blopped* forkfuls of dough onto a baking sheet. With Pillsbury, I rapped the can on a corner of the counter, twisted it open, extracted the biscuits, placed them on a pan, and baked. My biscuits did not taste like Bisquick or Pillsbury. What was wrong with my biscuits was not my biscuits but my attachment to having them taste like something out of my childhood, which had come out of a box or a can. My biscuits didn't!

When I next made biscuits, I decided to taste the biscuits of *today*: light, flaky, buttery, wheaty, sunny, earthy, vibrant, melt in your mouth. Letting go of fixed views, the reality of today appears—and you can work with it. What is it to be a man or to be a woman? A man or a woman awake today? Taste and know. What is it to be you? You yourself, beyond compare?

So when Zen Master Tenkei says, "See with your eyes. Smell with your nose. Taste with your tongue. Nothing in the universe is hidden. What else would you have me say?"—please, try it out. The Zen master wants to liberate you from your unattainable preoccupation with perfection, to encourage you to actually have your experience, and to empower you to respond based on your experience. Taste with your tongue, think your thoughts, feel your feelings. Have your life. And people object, "But suppose it's not right?" "Suppose I don't like it?" "Suppose others complain?" You'll have to weather it, and see what you can learn: some successes, some failures, a work in progress. As Zen Master Yakusan said, "Awkward in a hundred ways, clumsy in a thousand, still I go on."

~

The Ceremony of Eating
Just One Potato Chip

If you have the spirit of "not dwelling in the realm of right and wrong," how can this not be the practice of directly entering unsurpassable wisdom?

ZEN MASTER DŌGEN

Tasting what you put in your mouth may be a challenge, but you will be right in the heart of things, right in the "increasing depths of your life," as the poet Rilke says, "where it calmly gives out its secret." Several years ago, I conducted a silent, focused, mindful tasting of potato chips (you *can* eat just one!), oranges, and Hydrox cookies (they are, or were, vegetarian, whereas Oreos had some animal fat at the time).

On this occasion about a dozen of us participated (I've also done this ceremony with more than two hundred people at a single sitting, and one fourteen-ounce bag sufficed for the room). We started by eating one potato chip, which is a fascinating, unheard-of, esoteric practice—the Ceremony of Eating Just One Potato Chip. We rarely give our entire attention to a potato chip, as we are busy talking, watching TV, or using crisp and crunch and grease and salt to go unconscious—that is, not to think, feel, worry, or stress.

After tasting a chip with concentration, focus, and mindfulness, one person said: "An instant of salt and grease and then a tasteless pulp in my mouth. If I wasn't paying attention, I would have thought there was something there that I was missing and gone on trying to get the experience that wasn't there in the first place." So we could modify the old adage "you can never get enough of what you don't really want" to "you can never get enough of what's not actually there." Still, it will take fine-tuning your awareness to realize this. When our awareness is not clearly present while we eat, we do not notice that what we want is not to be found, and that eating more, aiming for fulfillment, we become full yet sadly unsatisfied.

This is not an easy lesson to learn, so we often need a structured setting in order to observe our experience more carefully than we might otherwise. Once when I announced this Ceremony of Eating Just One Potato Chip, a young man leapt to his feet and yelled out, "You're crazy!" "That," I pontificated, "is why this is a ceremony—we don't expect you to do this at home on your own."

Sometimes a participant will comment, "I'd forgotten how delicious a potato chip is." You are welcome, of course, to have your own experience.

When we tasted the oranges, people were ecstatic with their praise and delight: "So refreshing!" "Sweet and juicy!" "Amazing!" "Succulent!" "Tingly!" "Satisfying." "Thoroughly enjoyable!"

When we went on to the cookies, I couldn't believe it: most people refused to finish a whole cookie. Some even refused to taste it. After really tasting an orange, people's awareness was alert and receptive enough to notice all that was artificial, overly sweet, and chemical flavored in the cookie. With their heightened awareness, people found nothing there worth eating, so the cookies were set aside. Turning them down was not a matter of willpower or dieting. The commercial cookies were set aside by the power of clear discernment, which was based on tasting what you put in your mouth. Buddhism sometimes calls clear discernment "wisdom."

Often we have a habit of not tasting what we put in our mouths. We have more important things to be doing! Actually, stopping to taste would interrupt our thinking, planning, and judging, and it may seem vitally important to listen to this beloved inner voice, even though it is the voice Michael Singer, in *The Untethered Soul*, calls "your bad roommate" who won't stop talking. When we actually stop our inner voice long enough to taste, we might experience something unpleasant. So the habit of not tasting may be based on an implicit understanding that to be on the safe side, it's best not to taste too closely.

Of course, limiting our awareness to avoid unpleasant experiences means that we will also not notice what is pleasurable and deeply nourishing. We can't get the nourishment without chancing the distaste! No wonder people like commercial foods—they're so predictable. No risk. No possibility of experiencing something distasteful. And all too often, no vitality, no real life—in other words, no wilderness!

Fast foods or commercial products are designed to captivate or hook you with their initial flavor sensations, but as you continue to chew and taste, somehow not much is there. Oranges, apples, walnuts, lettuces—these foods have little impact initially, but as you chew and taste, the flavors expand, deepen, rush, quicken, cascade. As the flavors come alive in your tasting, so do you.

When we actually taste something, anything, we come alive inside. When we are not tasting, being alive and able to eat can become a bother rather than a blessing. Much of our life may go by, and what will we show up for and actually experience? Closely. Intimately. Remember: You're alive! You're the cook!

8

SEEKING THE WAY

Work in the kitchen may take many forms, but fundamentally it means giving the objects of awareness your attention—that is, the use of your consciousness to help the ingredients realize their true potential. You quickly find that giving out directives only goes so far—the ingredients do not simply obey—but that asking for direction moves the meal forward. How would you like to be cooked? What needs doing next? You listen, you taste, you feel. You work with your hands to help them be handy, with your body to be grounded and fully manifested. You work with ingredients so that they may be offered as food. Your work with thoughts is to do some disentangling so that the one thought needed steps forward on its cue. You study feelings enough that they are no longer a stain on your persona and instead in-form your being with what we call soul. You're getting cooked, along with the food.

Way-Seeking Mind

True suffering, also, is fundamentally always a prayer . . . True effort of the will, i.e. one-hundred-percent effort, true work, is also a prayer. When it is intellectual work, it is prayer. Hallowed be thy name. When it is creative effort, it is prayer. Thy kingdom come. When it is work with a view to supplying for the material needs of life, it is prayer: Give us this day our daily bread. And all these forms of prayer in the language of work have their corresponding benedictions or graces.

ANONYMOUS IN *MEDITATIONS ON THE TAROT*

In order to make reverential offerings, there is a position called tenzo. Since ancient times this position has been held by accomplished monks who have way-seeking mind, or by senior disciples with an aspiration for enlightenment. This is so because the position requires wholehearted practice. Those without way-seeking mind will not have good results, in spite of their efforts.

ZEN MASTER DŌGEN

Along with other Zen teachers, Zen Master Dōgen has emphasized the importance of *way-seeking mind*. That is to say, fulfilling one's life purpose is not only acquiring knowledge and skills but also opening your perceptual awareness and your capacity to respond in the present moment from your inner depths, or seeking the way to be awake in the present moment. As one Zen master said, "If you memorize slogans, you are unable to make subtle adaptations according to the situation . . . If you stick to your teacher's school and memorize slogans, this is not enlightenment: it is a part of intellectual knowledge."

In our world, there are the cultural norms, expectations, and standards. Beyond that, you'll need to keep finding out as much as you can and finally have the courage and where-withal to express what comes from within. The cooks in the wonderful Netflix *Chef's Table* series realize this. Beyond absorbing the traditional ways to cook, they eventually realize that they wish to go out on their own and cook food their way (often using local produce). Then the results of their efforts deeply touch people.

Suzuki Roshi's advice was not to stick to anything. You don't know what will happen next. In one episode of *Chef's Table*, an Italian chef, Massimo, tells his chef to go ahead and serve a whole tray of broken tarts that had been dropped on the floor. Now breaking the tarts is done on purpose, and the dish is called Oops, I Dropped the Lemon Tart!

Seeking the way is both outwardly and inwardly oriented. We want to find out the way to cook rice or the way to make a salad dressing. We want to discover how to work with less stress, how to focus our energy, how to work with our emotions, and more intimately, perhaps, the way to be true to ourselves, or the way to express our heart. Cookbooks tend to provide the instructions for working with the materials, while working with yourself will largely be up to you. Much of the time we do not realize that self-work is a possibility, so we may start believing, "I'm just not much of a cook," or, "I'm not meant to cook." Putting your heart into what you are doing is often an important step along the way.

No one has been you before, and no one will ever be you again. You're a work in progress, with various aims and agendas, goals and ambitions, dreams, hopes, and fears. What will see you through is cultivating this mind that *seeks the way*, or what Suzuki Roshi called, most famously, *beginner's mind*. You continue to find out how to do things, how to seek inwardly as well as outwardly.

"True work," we learn in *Meditations on the Tarot*, "is also a prayer." It may be formed or formless—what is the way to express what is innermost? The text also states that work means "learning the art of learning." May I bring through what is from Beyond? Again from *Meditations on the Tarot*: "Learn at first concentration without effort; transform work into play; make every yoke that you have accepted easy and every burden that you carry light!"

There is work to accomplishing this—working on how we work. Even choosing to work is to sacrifice other possible activities so that we can focus on the work at hand. Our awareness engaged in work tends to be accessible to the Sacred coming through, perhaps more so than letting our awareness be unoccupied. Way-seeking mind is busy—be it walking, working, dancing, singing—and yet open to inspiration, insight, or reworking.

If using favored cookbooks is what makes cooking satisfying and enjoyable for you, you may have no need to look further. When you are ready for something else, chances are it will appear.

Way-Seeking Spinach

You might think that you are a terrific cook, but now it's time to do something else. You might think you are a terrible cook, but now you have something else to do. A good cook is someone who continues to study how to be a good cook.

A PARAPHRASE OF ONE OF SUZUKI ROSHI'S TEACHINGS

I'll never forget a time when I was the tenzo at Tassajara and we had a case of spinach—twenty-four bunches—to prepare for dinner. As I had never before cooked spinach, I was concerned about having it come out the way it should. I looked in several cookbooks, but none of them explained how to cook spinach so that you ended up with *spinach* rather than spanakopita, spinach lasagna, or spinach soufflé. In time it became obvious that you *cook* it—apply heat over time—but along the way, there were so many uncertainties.

I don't know that my mother ever cooked spinach, and if she did, she didn't show me how you do it. Along with so many other mothers, mine occasionally heated up frozen spinach—these days, who knows what is getting microwaved or baked from the freezer—and even the few mothers who cooked spinach might not have had a very good method. I never went to cooking school, but friends who have tell me that you are primarily taught how to work with the flesh of animals: how to prepare pâtés and sausages, how to cut up carcasses. How do you actually learn something about cooking spinach?

My friends who went to acupuncture school say that what you learn in class is how to pass the state examination. Once you've leaped through that hoop, you begin studying how to do acupuncture, on patients. There's a certain irony with this, as acupuncture emphasizes using the close experience of sensory information to diagnose the patient and having something of a poetic imagination, which is attuned both to classic procedures and to insight arising on the occasion to what is *beyond knowing*. (Reading Abraham Verghese's *Cutting for Stone*, you find out that Western medicine has a body of knowledge about how to diagnose through direct observation as well, which from his perspective is underutilized. Last I heard, he was teaching these skills to medical students at Stanford University.)

Can you trust that—human awareness and responsiveness? You bet you can. In fact, the more you do so in cooking, the more your food will come alive. You see, smell, taste, and dream up what to do with the ingredients presented. You connect your experience of what is outside (the ingredients) with what is inside (your intention, knowledge, and experience) and what is from Beyond (your insight, intuition, imagination). Sometimes it's called magic.

I can't say that we performed magic with our spinach. We cut the spinach at the base of the bunch, and we knew to wash it more than once, as spinach at that time tended to be quite muddy. Meanwhile, some of us began working on removing the stems. I had read that you were to fold the sides of the spinach leaves forward and hold them together with one hand, while you pulled the stem off, up the back of the leaf, with the other. No stem is left! Precisely following these instructions, you end up with exquisitely delicate spinach harboring not a trace of stem. The book said to do this. We complied.

Hence, several of us were busily engaged in religiously removing stems, leaf by leaf, by hand, when someone said, "Ed, I just tried eating a stem, and it's not tough at all. Why don't we leave them on? If the stems are this tender when they are raw, they will only get more tender as they cook."

What is the way to prep spinach for cooking? I tried a stem or two—tender enough to chew easily. "Okay, let's leave the stems," was my conclusion. The kitchen exploded with a huge sigh of relief that sounded like a burst of cheering.

What is the way to prep spinach? It all depends, doesn't it? What dish are you planning to make with the spinach? Who are you cooking for? How much help do you have? Do you have any other plans for the afternoon?

If you want to make a spinach soufflé or timbale soft and smooth, the way to do that is to remove the stems laboriously or use a Cuisinart with the sieve attachment. Even then, you'll probably want to remove the largest, gnarliest stems, which can be much more stringy than the others. Are your diners people who demand food without the work of chewing? Are they ready and willing, even eager, to apply rules and standards? Or are they more country folk, down-to-earth eaters who are prepared to dig in, chew, and swallow, to enjoy with gusto? And even if you wish to offer the more refined version of cooked spinach, do you have the help and the time to carry it out? What is the way?

Having tried a variety of methods and usually serving people who enjoy eating while not being overly preoccupied with assessing their food, I've come to my way. I cut the clump of spinach twice, once close to the base of the stems and a second time at the base of the largest leaves. Remove the loose stems and use for stock; save the large leaves that were above the second cut and the smaller leaves that were hidden among the stems. Wash thoroughly, as needed—nowadays the spinach we purchase is not nearly as muddy as it was in the sixties, unless you're buying from a farmers' market or CSA (Community Supported Agriculture).

When the stems of the spinach are primarily of the thinner variety, I might just cut the spinach at its base, spot and pull out those few leaves that are the largest, and cut the stems off of those—eating the other stems along with the leaves.

For cooking? I usually melt a bit of butter in the bottom of the pan, add the spinach and some salt, cover, and apply heat over time.

What is the way? The way is to study the way each step of the way.

~

To Cut or Not to Cut the Collards

One morning I went to work in the kitchen at a well-known Zen center. We were instructed to tear collard greens—four cases—that is, to tear them after cutting the leafy part off of the stem. Of course, tearing rather than cutting collard greens is going to take two to three times as long, since you can cut several together while you tear one at a time. Is tearing rather than cutting worth that much extra time? I didn't think so, so I asked why we were tearing the collards. The answer was a holy "At this center we *tear* the collards." We were not given a reason (more tender, more beautiful—and significantly, so that it warrants the extra work). No reason was given to waste hours of everyone's time.

I went into the kitchen and asked the assistant head cook, "Chef, may we have your permission to cut the collards rather than tearing them?"

"Sure."

So I went back outside to the prep area, mentioned that the assistant head cook in the kitchen had given his permission, and we cut collards until the break. After the break, when I was no longer there, the outside supervisor said, "Now that Edward is gone, we will be tearing the collards!" Enough already of all that disobedience! Back to doing it by the book, as written by the one in charge.

As for those torn collard greens (with a few cut ones)? After being washed in unicorn tears, they were served in the dining room with two dals and a spongy pancake. Two women from Ethiopia loved it! The greens were bitter and tough—just barely steamed. The hours of extra work tearing them instead of cutting them did not make any perceptible difference: they were bitter and tough! *Please*, I wondered, *would someone be willing to study which differences make a difference?*

That meal was three carbs and bitter, tough greens. It was August, summertime. What about summer vegetables: zucchini, green beans, peppers, eggplant, crookneck, tomatoes? What about fruits? Nuts? Cheeses? What about sauces? Seasonings? What about garnishes? What about sweet, sour, pungent? What about cooking the collards longer and seasoning them with garlic butter or a lemon-flavored peanut sauce? What about cooking the collards in a spicy ancho chili tomato sauce? What about being less bound by the rules and more waking up to how to cook?

Noticing differences and considering which differences make a difference, we study what is truly important in the kitchen. The laboriously torn collard greens were not a noticeable improvement over cut collards: that simple. I do not find this complicated: observe, study, find out. Try them both ways. Taste them side by side, and find a way to cook them so that they are tender, juicy, and flavorful.

Lovely Energy in the Kitchen

*If you encourage yourself with complete sincerity, you will
want to exceed monks of old in wholeheartedness and ancient
practitioners in thoroughness. The way for you to attain this
is by trying to make a fine cream soup for three cents
in the same way that monks of old could make
a broth of wild grasses for that little.*

ZEN MASTER DŌGEN

I became friends with Dennis who was cooking at Esalen
Institute many years ago. What an immense transition it had
been for him, coming from the Culinary Institute of America
where he had worked previously. At the Institute, everything is
structured, including a clear chain of command: "Chef, what
shall I do next?" Whatever it is, peeling potatoes, slicing carrots, washing spinach, the answer is, "Yes, chef, I will."

In contrast, during those days at Esalen, anyone could call
a time-out at any time: "I need a check-in" or "I'd like a
weather report." The whole kitchen would pause and regroup,
perhaps on the lawn outside, to form a therapy circle. What's
happening with you, and how do you feel about that? When
you've been in a chain of command focused on accomplishing
the work at hand, to drop everything and postpone cooking
until further notice can challenge your self-esteem if not your
sanity. Dennis said that it took awhile, but he did get more
used to it.

Someone needs to put up a sign for the retreatants: "Dinner
postponed until further notice," or "Dinner when we get

around to it," or "Dinner when we resolve our childhood trauma and residual anger."

Of course, I am in the school of putting emotions to work—not being immobilized by them and not acting them out, but putting emotions to work. As I often say, if I had to be completely loving while I was cooking, we would never have had anything to eat. I say, Turn it all into food! Transform everything! Zen monks are said to have mouths like a furnace (burning up everything) and minds like a fan in winter (completely useless). Instead of trying to sort things out with your thinking mind, turn the emotional energy into food!

Dennis said that one of his teachers at the Institute would come up to you while you were working and ask, "Chef, what are you making?" If you said, "Carrot soup," the instructor would ask, "And what should carrot soup taste like?" The correct answer was carrots.

Without careful study, we may conclude that adding ginger, green chilies, fresh cilantro or basil, and perhaps some lemon juice will make the carrot soup "so much more flavorful." "Isn't that delicious?" we say. Yes, the flavors are intense and perhaps beautifully vibrant, yet the original flavor may be masked. And since the orange color may signify carrot, winter squash, or yam, someone tasting the soup may ask, "What kind of soup is this?" Somewhat less or fewer of the same seasonings may bring out the best in the soup.

Classic French vegetable soups often seem to have carrot or cauliflower, say, sautéed with onion or leek, simmered with chicken stock, blended, finished with cream, and seasoned to taste. Perhaps a fresh herb garnish or small croutons as well. The chicken stock and cream give the soup a flavorful, reassuring body, which is carrot flavored. What's delicious is the chicken stock and cream—you can't beat it. Yet as a cook, especially if you are vegetarian or vegan, you train yourself to study whether it is possible to make a carrot soup that tastes even more like carrot—rather than the version where the carrot flavor is softened with the chicken stock and cream.

Perhaps your leftover oatmeal or cream of rice cereal can provide body and sweetness that do not soften the wild vegetable nature of carrot as much as the chicken stock and cream do. Perhaps you try using even more carrot to make the same quantity of soup, or you soften the carrot flavor a bit with stewed apple. Yellow onion, red onion, leek, shallot? You'll need to decide which of the onion family strikes a chord with carrot.

9

LET THINGS COME AND
ABIDE IN YOUR HEART

Presence meeting presence manifests when you study how
presence meets presence and practice meeting presence.
Strategies and scheming are of no avail. You simply meet
face-to-face, not knowing what will happen. Of course,
cooking is not the only activity where devotion brings worth
and fulfillment. Blessings come into our life when we work
at our craft whether it is cooking, gardening, woodworking,
dancing, acting. Whether it is doctoring, lawyering, pain
management, communication skills, parenting. Still, if you
are missing what is sacred, you could find yourself longing
for genuine connection: presence meeting presence in
complete stillness, like your baby sleeping—precious. What
is sacred is you yourself, your pure essence inside. And
a spiritual life is one where you engage essence, or True
Nature, with the outer world, the presence that is in other
people and things. What is unscripted appears, just as it is,
and you work with it, collaborating.

Receiving Flavors

In the art of cooking, the essential consideration
is to have a deeply sincere and respectful mind regardless
of the fineness or coarseness of the materials.

ZEN MASTER DŌGEN

These days when I taste attentively, the outer world often disappears; whole worlds are there in the tasting, like range after range of the distant blue mountains. In addition to sweet, sour, salty, pungent, and bitter, something mysterious appears: a stillness, a quiet presence, is right here in each moment, awaiting our receptive attention.

This is one aspect of Dōgen's teaching to "let things come and abide in your heart, and let your heart return and abide in things." When you allow for an intimate meeting with the world, the world awakens your heart. Dōgen puts the emphasis on relationship, or connection, as most basic to our happiness and well-being rather than the expediency of handling things objectively or by the book. Letting flavors come home to your heart is also counter to the understanding that we can be most happy when we do not need to relate with anything—the proverbial lying on the beach or stretching out with the remote in front of the telly, nothing to care for or to tend to. Often it is not our habit to let things come and abide in our hearts, yet we can grow into it.

I began, as we all did, with the tasting of my childhood, which was primarily focused on "I like it," or "I don't like it"—"I'll eat it," or "I won't eat it." This could be called our original taste-aesthetic: the foods we naturally turned toward and the ones we turned away from. At my cooking classes, I often have people introduce themselves by telling us about their favorite childhood foods. Often the descriptions include "my mother" or "my grandmother." As children, many of us shared similar creaturely sensibilities. We loved potatoes, mashed potatoes and gravy; pancakes, pancakes with syrup, pancakes with apple sauce; noodles, spaghetti and meat balls; cakes, layered cakes, birthday cakes; cream, whipped cream, ice cream. We didn't appreciate eggplant, mushrooms, mushy vegetables, avocados, Brussels sprouts. We turned toward sweet and away from bitter. It can be years—or never—before we discover IPAs and 70 or 85 percent dark chocolate—the bracing elixir of bitter.

As children, some of us may have put liver under our napkin or a sibling's napkin to escape having to eat it. Sometimes it wasn't just the flavor but also the texture that could be off-putting. I didn't want rubbery, as mushrooms could be, or buttery, the way avocados are, or even leafy, as lettuce was. What was there to chew on? Besides, with the salad dressing, lettuce was way too sharp or acidic. I started eating salad after a classmate in eighth grade brought in lettuce for show-and-tell, dressed with sour cream mixed with dried basil. My mom adopted the recipe.

When I think about it now, perhaps I wanted food to behave the way I had learned to behave: "Sit still and keep your mouth shut (unless you can say something pleasant)." It seemed that the big people were essentially asking, "Please don't make me have to experience you." And wasn't that what I wanted with my food? Little flavor, little taste, and please, nothing that I need to relate with and make a decision about. "Just try it," people say, and the answer is, "No, I would rather not experience anything unusual, anything outside what I know and know that I like."

Some of us manage to maintain our childhood aesthetic indefinitely. Others of us develop acquired tastes, and as we grow and mature, trying out new foods and flavors, our aesthetic changes. The criteria for tasting get reformulated. We're no longer in basic survival mode. We might even yearn to experience something new, something different. How about an adventure in flavor?

Another basic mode of tasting (or of experiencing anything) is to judge whether the food meets your standards—that is, your own likes and dislikes or your own sense of what is acceptable. Does your food measure up? When you are focused on meeting and surpassing the standards, you will frequently sense the impossibility of doing so. The more you focus on tasting the flavors of today, the more you relax your grip on maintaining the standards.

Of course, aiming for the stars of approval that will put you on the culinary map means you will probably need a well-developed sense of the markers—or a finely honed confidence in your own aesthetic.

Viewing taste standards as objective reality means that every meal becomes a test of whether your performance measures up, whether your food is acceptable. You could easily fail even after putting forth great effort. So we may turn to convenience foods that will predictably be the way you expect—always the same.

For many years, I cooked by generating a picture of how things should be and worked to make the food come out that way. I longed for recognition, for acclaim, and I thought I could get it by meeting and surpassing recognized taste-pictures.

And I was decent enough at this, though if you look back at my earlier cookbooks, you'll see that my taste was rather primitive. *Tassajara Cooking* recommended salt for flavoring food with barely a mention of sour or tart—lemon, lime, vinegar—or piquant or pungent—peppers, chilies, garlic, ginger. I was tasting what I put in my mouth to see if it measured up to a preestablished concept. What should it taste like? Does it, or doesn't it? And my preestablished concepts, or pictures, were close to what I'd grown up with.

The world of flavor opened up when I began to let tastes come and abide in my heart.

Developing a Palate as a Busboy at Greens

Our original mind includes everything within itself. It is always rich and sufficient within itself. You should not lose your self-sufficient mind. This does not mean a closed mind, but actually an empty mind and a ready mind. If your mind is empty, it is always ready for anything; it is open to everything.
SUZUKI ROSHI

Tasting what I put in my mouth underwent a major revitalization when I became a busboy at Greens Restaurant, the vegetarian restaurant that the San Francisco Zen Center opened in 1979. Baby lettuce salads with high-quality olive oil and champagne wine vinegar; black bean chili served on top of grated Jack cheese, with a flavorful and vibrant garnish of crème fraiche, thinly cut canned green chili strips, and whole cilantro leaves; grilled vegetables—and even fruit!—including peppers, asparagus, peaches, as well as brochettes with marinated tofu; a wine list from which you could select and enjoy by the glass—very common today, but at the time it was primarily house white or house red. (Diners did not know what to make of it—you mean I have to pick?)

When we opened, Greens was at the forefront of restaurant cuisine, serving its lively offerings while others still served iceberg-lettuce salads in puddles of dressing, house wines, and steamed vegetables (often overcooked), using their grills only for meat.

Deborah Madison's culinary brilliance, as the founding chef at Greens, brought it all to life. For me and for her many new fans, the world of taste opened up and kept opening up. Apples were not just apples, they were Braeburns or Granny Smith, and you could taste the difference. Food embodied so many more possibilities. When you took the time and attention to taste, truly taste, food was not just food, not just fuel for the human body, but an exciting new world. Sensations sparkled and danced in your mouth, beyond any idea, any conception, any previous picture. Looking back now, I am reminded of Dōgen's teaching, "When you attain realization, you do not think, *Aha! Realization! Just as I expected.*" Thank you, Deborah! Not at all what I expected, but rather cuisine alive and full-flavored. Reality itself beyond our picturing, beyond our expectations.

Frisée, endive, fresh black mission figs, Sharlyn melons, breads from our Tassajara Bread Bakery, a Nicoise pizza with slivers of whole lemon, so that perhaps not with every bite, but occasionally, sunlight exploded in your awareness. Chèvre, the soft creamy goat cheese, appeared in pizzas, pastas, and salads. Eggplant was elevated, sometimes arriving at the table baked in a saffron custard.

After all those years of Zen cooking, largely by the book, it was revelation. You put something in your mouth, and if you were tasting, you went straight to heaven. Pasta from the Fettuccine Brothers, fresh yet somehow *al dente*, as they worked to add the maximum amount of flour to their pastas; filo from Scheherazade, made by hand; and lettuces fresh from the Zen Center's Green Gulch Farm.

Letting flavors come home to your heart, or welcoming sensations, contrasts with our more customary way of giving out instructions and directives to the objects of our awareness—telling them how to behave and then assessing them for how well they meet what are essentially our wishful demands for compliance with our internal standards. When you open up to receive taste, you are no longer imposing your wishes on reality but experiencing how magical things can be. You begin to notice and participate in the creation of the experience by letting your awareness be in-formed, or shaped, by your meeting. The world shifts from black and white to color. Where is that music coming from? *Let things come and abide in your heart, and let your heart return and abide in things.*

Some of our students wondered: Was Greens really Zen? Shouldn't we have started a soup kitchen? Were the prices too high? Don't we have standards?

It was genius, Deborah's genius with food, shared by those working with her. It was also Richard Baker Roshi's genius for creating dynamic space: envisioning how an old warehouse with frosted-glass windows could be transformed into a light and airy dining room and bringing in the giant redwood burl and carved redwood tables of J. B. Blunk, the lively paintings of Edward Avedisian and the spacious ones of Willard Dixon. And it was devotion, the energetic devotion, of a stream of Zen students. Hard work sparked by vision. Equally astonishing.

At Work with Wines

*Read each sentence with a fresh mind. You should not say,
"I know what Zen is," or "I have attained enlightenment."
This is also the real secret of the arts: always be a beginner.*

SUZUKI ROSHI

After serving as a busboy and waiter at Greens, eventually I
became the manager and wine buyer. In this capacity, I began
tasting wines with a convivial group of tasters who were friends
of the restaurant, including Dick Graff, who was making
world-class chardonnays and pinot noirs at his Chalone
Winery, east of Soledad, California, in the Pinnacles. Greens
staff members Deborah Madison, Jim Phalan, and Renee des
Tombes joined in as well. We would taste six to nine wines of
the same varietal.

At these tastings, I came to discover that taste was both
shared and arbitrary. When we had wines that were of distinctly differing quality, our tasters would agree on which were
well made and which were obviously flawed. When the wines
were of equal quality, however, liking or disliking became
arbitrary, and the experts did not agree. A wine that tasted
like straw for one person would remind someone else of the
afternoon sun dipping toward the ocean, shining on the dry
California hillsides dotted with oaks. I soon discovered that
one person's Kool-Aid could be someone else's strawberry with
hints of rhubarb.

In those days, Greens had a very small wine list, partly due
to limited storage and partly due to a philosophy of selectivity.

David Crane, who helped us identify wines for tasting, exemplified this by saying, "Hundreds of bad wines have passed my lips, so that only the best need pass yours." So we wanted to study which wines we liked by themselves—"Such hard work," we joked! And then we wanted to know which wines best complemented our vegetarian food. For instance, Louis Martini cabernet sauvignon and zinfandel never measured up to more expensive wines when tasted side by side. Yet these same robust, flavorful—sometimes even *chewy*—reds that surpassed the Martini wines in side by side tastings would consistently overwhelm our vegetarian food, whereas the Martini reds came alive with our food and brought out more flavors. Decent! Harmonious! Friendly!

Unpretentious, no-name wines can shine at the expense of their priccy brethren.

The bigger, more full-bodied wines may grab your attention more easily, but beyond the usual assessment of wines, carefully tasting what you eat and drink, sensing what enhances what, you may find, as I did, that you enjoy companionable wines in a lower price range.

Trying out wines one after another, then tasting each wine with each dish: asparagus soup garnished with tarragon butter or crème fraiche and chervil; charcoal-grilled vegetables and marinated tofu brochettes with brown rice slathered with herb-mustard butter; a pizza, say, with chipotle sauce on the bottom, cheese, tomatoes, green pepper slices, garnished with cilantro; another with perhaps four cheeses and freshly chopped herbs on top; a pasta of the day, perhaps fettuccine with fresh peas and thinly sliced stewed leeks, garlic, cream, and lemon zest, with perhaps roasted chopped walnuts on top. Which pairings sang well together? Which were the most enjoyable?

Dick Graff was especially helpful as a tutor. One of the California pioneers who used French oak to age his Chalone chardonnay and pinot noir, he was an unusually brilliant man, equally warmhearted and exacting—an artist, an engineer, an intellectual, and a *worker*. I can't remember for sure, but I think he built (or re-assembled) the organ that he once played for us at Chalone. His energy scrubbing out a huge stainless-steel wine-fermenting tank (room-sized) reminded me of Katagiri Roshi running bent over to polish the zendo floor. His wines seemed to reflect his character as well: on one hand, well structured, and on the other, singing praises—while other wines often seemed noteworthy for being stately, robust, by the book, or overly voluptuous.

Dick would coach me, "Ed, this Joseph Phelps has a grassiness that is distinctly sauvignon blanc. Catalog it." Once he invited us to his house at Chalone: Deborah, Dan Welch, and me. We had roasted chicken with his 1980 chardonnay; the juicy bird accented the wine's delicate high notes of butterscotch, cloves, and vanilla—catalog it! Following the chicken course, small plates of watercress salad appeared and surprisingly a new wine —the 1978 Chalone Pinot Noir—and new, larger wine glasses. Having no idea what that wine might bring to the table, I swirled it in my glass and sniffed. "Oh my God," I mumbled to myself and burst into tears: from the depths of the earth, definitely feminine, a mossy, lush, forest path, with mushrooms, delicate fruit, perhaps raspberry, and a knowing that arises spontaneously, "I am loved." Catalog it!

To catalog it is to commit an experience to memory, to note it, to file it away. Then it is yours and becomes a basis for informing your aesthetic and your intuition. When you need it, it appears—or you scan through your memory banks to find it. Without cataloging, it's simply no longer available at a later time. You have less of your experience to draw on, to in-form you.

Breaking the Trance of Routine

To exist in big mind . . . is to believe that something is
supporting us and supporting all our activities . . . All these
things are supported by something big that has no form or
color. It is impossible to know what it is, but something
exists there, something that is neither material nor spiritual.
Something like that always exists, and we exist in that space.

SUZUKI ROSHI

Sometimes when we eat and feel love, we call that comfort food, the food we grew up with—it's pleasant and we don't have to taste. Nothing there to confront our taste buds with bad news. Other times, it's as though something is coming through from Beyond: vast stillness, luminous presence, warmheartedness. It is not a thing actually, but as Suzuki Roshi put it: "Something is there, something large . . . and we exist in that space." As long as you exist in that space, you are held, and you have a place at the table of life.

Largely this experience depends not on the food but on your tasting, whether in a zendo *oryoki* meal, at home, in an upscale restaurant, or with fast food.

Sometimes people wonder, *Is that Zen?* Are you allowed revelation in Zen, or will you steadfastly stick to experiencing things as they are and always have been, the trance of everyday life? Will you taste something from Beyond? "Subtle feeling," it is said in one koan, "reveals illumination."

As I've continued teaching cooking classes over the years, I have devoted more time to having students taste a dish in the course of adding one ingredient at a time. Now it's about tasting sweet, sour, salt, pungent, and bitter. It's about tasting earth, stem and leaf, flower and fruit. What makes the dish what it is?

Along with my students, I too started tasting more carefully, more intimately. *Speak to me,* I say. *Share with me your song, your prayer, your secrets. Instead of telling you how you should taste, I will listen to how you do taste. And connecting with my heart, I will let you move me.* It has only taken thirty-five to forty years.

⟶

A Salad of Five Flavors

Regulations for Zen Monasteries states, "If the six tastes are not suitable and if the food lacks the three virtues, the tenzo's offering to the assembly is not complete."
ZEN MASTER DŌGEN IN *INSTRUCTIONS FOR THE COOK*

One New Year's, my next-door neighbor Jennifer was inspired to share with me her intention to learn more about cooking vegetables and preparing salads. A few days later, she phoned and said that she would like a consultation with the food doctor: "I followed your instructions, but it's not that great. Would you be willing to help me?"

"Absolutely, Jennifer, I'd be most willing."

"Can I come over now?"

"Come on over now."

And soon enough, there was Jennifer standing in the window of the back door to my kitchen, bowl of salad in hand. In she came.

I have wonderful neighbors—not on any measureable scale, simply in terms of my love and gratitude. Mark has fixed roof leaks on my house, and he has the ladders you need to get up onto the roof! I love having capable men around. I don't even have a basement, let alone a ladder. When I discovered a huge puddle an inch deep sopping the rugs in the downstairs bathroom (how does water seep through concrete?), Mark answered my call.

No leaks were apparent to me, but Mark said that he would check the shut-off valves. While he reached down under the sink to do so, I said, "But they aren't dripping." His hand reappeared with water on his fingertips. "Look at that," he said. "Usually if you turn the valve on all the way, it stops leaking," and so it did. You learn a lot by seeing with your eyes and exploring with your hands—and not just in the kitchen.

Jennifer had prepared one of my hand-fried kale salads, where you start by cutting the kale—dino kale is the easiest to cut and has bright, fresh green flavor—into julienne strips crosswise, then sprinkle on salt, and squeeze in your hands until moisture appears and the kale is limp rather than crisp. Yum! Jennifer had added some dried cranberries and toasted chopped almonds.

After tasting Jennifer's salad, I said, "Yeah, you're right—the flavors are muddy, aren't they?"

"Yes, it's indistinct. Blah! Nothing. What does it need?"

Attentively tasting another bite, I gave my verdict: "Pretty much everything. Let's start with more salt, and we can go through each ingredient, one by one, so that you'll be able to tell what a difference each one makes. Make sure you have a clear taste-picture of where we are starting from."

"Got it," says Jennifer, pinching a lump of kale and popping it into her mouth.

I sprinkle on a healthy pinch or two of salt from a dish by the side of the stove. Situated on a table in the corner of the kitchen, the salt is also readily available at the end of my work counter. "Real Salt," I pronounce (which is a brand name for salt from the Great Salt Lake), knowing that Jennifer uses it as well.

"Yeah," she says, "my kids can tell the difference now. We had something the other day with commercial salt, and they said, 'Mom, this has no flavor.'"

"Jennifer, you've ruined them for having an ordinary life with mediocre food."

My partner Margot from the next room briefly joins the conversation, and Jennifer is quick to respond, "I'm willing to pay the price."

"Start saving now," she continues, "for their therapy later. Your kids will find some way you failed them." ("Mom, you always used Real Salt, so now we can't enjoy ordinary food like everyone else. What were you thinking?")

Once the salt is on, I vigorously begin squeezing the kale using both hands, pausing now and again to reconfigure the contents of the bowl so that everything gets squeezed.

"Oh," Jennifer notices, "you really squeeze it, don't you? I wasn't using that much pressure."

"Yep, squeeze it like you mean it." Shortly, the kale appears moist and glistening, and I note that to Jennifer. "See how juicy the kale has become? The salt goes into the kale, which brings water out, and already you have some dressing. Plus the kale is easier to chew because water has been released. The water was keeping it crisp."

Of course, you don't do this with lettuce because you want the crispness, and you even soak the lettuce in water if you want more. You dry off the lettuce, and then (in my school) you put oil on first to give the lettuce a protective coating before putting on the salt and vinegar. Voila! The lettuce stays crisp. In this case, however, the kale became limp—flavorful and easier to chew.

Using a thumb and forefinger, we both take a taste of the salted kale: "It has flavor now," Jennifer remarks. "Yes," I add, "green, grassy, front of the mouth. Salt, I would say, focuses the flavor. If you were looking through a camera lens, the blur becomes distinct."

"You know there's salt," Jennifer shares, "but it's not salty."

"Exactly, and if you get too much salt, you can pour the water off or even rinse off the kale in a strainer, but I prefer not to need to do that, as you would also be pouring off flavor."

"And we want the flavor," Jennifer confirms.

"Yes," I affirm, "and salt is also like an invitation to your mouth that says, 'You're going to like this; give it a taste.' And you say, 'Yum!'"

"Of course, salt use is often overdone. For instance, with fast foods, your mouth gets excited by the salt, and there is so much that you do not really taste what is underneath it. You just want more salt, and keep eating. Salt is also used to mask poor ingredients, which is why chefs prefer unsalted butter—it tastes better, and salted butter is rumored to have more off-flavors disguised by the salt. Sometimes chefs over-use salt in their cooking because they are not using the tart or the pungent flavors that we will be adding shortly."

"Next we'll add some sweetness," I announce. "Would you like sugar or honey?"

Jennifer says she isn't sure, so I expound on the possibilities: "White sugar just adds sweetness, so it's great for enhancing the fruit flavors of fruit tarts. Honey is spring-blossom sweet, a flowery quality, although some honey is darker, more robust and earthy. Maple syrup gets things sweet with that faintly smoky essence of the North woods. With brown sugar, you're getting some molasses flavors."

"Couldn't this kale salad use some springtime?" Jennifer suggests.

I concur, "I'm with you." I pour in a couple spoonfuls of honey and clean off the lip of the jar. "Want to use your hands?" I ask.

While Jennifer mixes in the honey, I explain that generally you use about equal amounts of sweet and sour: sugar or honey and lemon juice, lime juice, or vinegar. "That's what we'll be adding next."

Using our fingers, we taste the kale. Not really having noticed any tightness, I nonetheless feel my body relaxing.

"That's sweet," Jennifer deadpans. "The flavors are softer."

"Yes," I agree, "softer, mellower, and don't you start feeling comfortable? Even with just that small amount of sweet, you get a little rush of pleasure; you feel happy."

We smile at each other, nodding: "Yep," we say, "that's good, good and satisfying."

"Sweet and sour and sweet and pungent are classic seasoning combinations," I elaborate. "We'll be doing both." After a pause, I remember to mention that if you get too much of any flavor from an ingredient or from the seasoning, you can always try adding some sugar to soften the effects—for instance, mashed potatoes (sweet carbohydrate) is one classic solution. (When the mashed potatoes are oversalted, you have a big problem.)

For the tartness—I'm equating this with sour or acidic, though definitions include bitter and pungent—I suggest that we add lime juice, and I retrieve a fresh lime from across the kitchen. Opening the top drawer of my work counter, I pull out my wooden juicer. This is the classic tool that has a handle at one end and the ridged, cone-shaped juicer at the other. After cutting the lime in half, I hold it in my left hand and twist the juicer back and forth with my right. I offer Jennifer the other half of the lime and the juicer. (The limes don't usually have seeds, but if you are juicing lemons, you can first squeeze the half lemon above the open palm of the opposite hand, and with the juice flowing between your fingers, catch and deposit any seeds in the compost. Then use the wooden juicer.)

We fold in the lime juice, using a rubber spatula, and then taste. When you haven't consciously tasted the transformation that tartness elicits, the first time can be taste opening, the way a vista can be eye opening.

Jennifer's excitement is palpable. "It's tingly in my mouth," she enthuses. "It's singing."

"Singing, bright, vibrant," I confirm, "what some people call the high note in flavors." My mouth is alive with sparkle. This is fun!

I mention to Jennifer that first thing in the morning for several months I have been drinking the juice of a lime or half a lemon with warm water—and almost immediately, I feel awake, a wondrous shift from groggy, heavy, and sluggish. Apparently, the acidity of the citrus shifts the body toward more alkaline, overcoming the effects of coffee, tea, alcohol, sugar—many of the items we may indulge in. I also note that the last time I read about tartness, there was uncertainty about whether the acidic quality stimulated the taste buds or simply removed their outermost layer, making the taste buds more sensitive. Either way, you taste more.

The acidic quality is known to be especially cleansing or refreshing when consuming fats or oils; hence, the vinegar to go along with the oil in salad dressings. This also accounts for the importance of adequate levels of acid in wines, which are otherwise considered "flat" or "flabby" and do not fulfill their function of refreshing the palate. Inadequate acid and excess sugar in wines become less noticeable when they are served ice-cold—have you noticed? In that case, you are refreshed more by the chill and less by the qualities of the wine.

On a high from the lime juice, Jennifer and I head on to the pungent: black pepper, red pepper, chilies, green chilies, fresh garlic, fresh ginger, mustard, horseradish. These flavors are warming in your mouth and contribute heat. "Let's use ginger," I say. "I really like it with kale," and I reach for it on my handy side table. Then from my equally handy top drawer, I take out my Chinese bamboo ginger grater. I start to grate, while explaining to Jennifer: "These graters are interesting because you grate on the upstroke rather than the down."

"But you don't have to peel the ginger?" Jennifer asks.

"No, not at all. Here. Give it a go," and I pass the grater and ginger over to her. After she has done some grating, I show her how to clean the grater by whapping it firmly on the counter. Holding it up, I let her see how free of ginger it is. "This is important," I pronounce, "if you grate a lot of ginger, you want an easy-to-clean grater, but if you don't have one, use your cheese grater."

We mix and taste. Jennifer is getting excited: "It's not just hotter—there's more flavor!"

"Yes, somehow the flavor is more full of flavor—the kale, the salt, the honey, the lime juice. All the flavors somehow expand and are more robust in the mouth. Not like habanero chili or cayenne hot, the added heat in our ginger-enhanced kale salad is not that hot, yet it seems to say, 'Take me seriously,' and we do. It gets our attention without inducing pain."

Jennifer is glowing, "This is amazing. It's wonderful."

"One more flavor to go"—I sound like a tour guide—"and that's the bitter flavor." Bitter is the least familiar flavor in our lexicon, so some examples are useful: dark chocolate, coffee, and tea have their bitter qualities, so we add dairy and sugar—one lump or two? There are bitter greens: escarole, frisée, collards, as well as red-purple radicchio. Yet the largest grouping here is nuts and seeds: walnuts, almonds, sunflower, sesame.

One useful note here is that people's sensitivity to bitter is variable. At a workshop once, paper tabs were passed out, which we were instructed to taste. This was in conjunction with genetic mapping. The speaker mentioned that people are genetically different in their capacity to sense bitter: 60 percent experience bitter; 20 percent find bitter extremely bitter, simply horrid (and butterscotch balls came to their rescue once they found out they were in this category); and 20 percent barely notice it. Without having to get a genetic map, I know I'm in the 60 percent that can readily tolerate and appreciate bitter. (If you want to be sure to not offend anyone, brew your beer sweet and light and sell milk chocolate.)

Pale ale and dark chocolate are finally earning market share, as the bitter quality offers taste, and we who love bitter find deep, dark, delicious fulfillment. The taste is that of earth, which can be either sweet earth or bitter earth. After sharing some of this with Jennifer, I ventured, "How about some toasted sesame seeds? They'll also provide good color for garnishing the top of the salad."

I reach for a small skillet and the jar of brown sesame seeds, sprinkle some into the skillet, turn on the flame, and begin roasting. Soon the seeds are popping and jumping, so I put on a lid, turn off the heat, and let them pop another half minute or so. Roasting seeds is like toasting bread: more nutty, toasty, earthy sweetness. Literally, with the heat, carbohydrates are converted into sugars.

Dotting the top of the kale salad, the seeds make a picturesque addition. Jennifer tastes her clump thoughtfully and comments, "It's as though it has ground now, a foundation. Brings it back down to earth."

"You got it," I tell her, "but not too much to bury all the rest. Keep in mind one last thing—that you might still want a garnish of green on top of the seeds. Shall we try one?"

Jennifer agrees, so I mention that I have green onion and fresh cilantro. We chiffonade some cilantro: bright, grassy, fresh. "It's singing a high note."

10

THE BLACK DRAGON JEWEL IS EVERYWHERE

Many believe that connection with Source and Sustenance is not in the kitchen but somewhere else that is more gripping, perhaps higher, more soaring, or less work with fewer obstacles. On occasion you may find engaging times elsewhere, losing yourself in what is bigger. I'm especially in awe of mountain climbers. One said recently, "Your state of mind eludes words." The intensity, the adrenaline rush, the high may be compelling, yet things that grab your attention often do not suffice to bring you up short, stopping you on the spot, so that you need to wake up or turn back. Watching television, going to the movies or the mall, surfing the internet, or going out for pizzas, beer, and burgers may fill the time and space, but while you were being carried along, where was your opportunity to show up? Resonating with what is innermost, you give it voice; you put it into action.

Is There Anything Good about Working in the Kitchen?

Do not wait for great enlightenment, as great enlightenment is the tea and rice of daily activity. Do not wish for beyond enlightenment, as beyond enlightenment is a jewel concealed in your hair.

ZEN MASTER DŌGEN

Zen Master Dōgen arrived in China in 1223, and while he was still on the boat, he made the acquaintance of a cook-monk who had walked perhaps ten miles to purchase dried mushrooms for an upcoming ceremony. Dōgen felt a strong and vibrant connection with him and wished to invite the cook-monk to share a meal with him, but the cook refused, saying he needed to attend to his responsibilities. Dōgen did not understand how he could be so committed to the work of the kitchen:

> I again asked the tenzo, "Honorable Tenzo, why don't you concentrate on zazen (meditation) practice and on the study of the ancient masters' words rather than troubling yourself by holding the position of tenzo and just working? Is there anything good about it?"
>
> The tenzo laughed a lot and replied, "Good man from a foreign country, you do not yet understand practice or know the meaning of the words of ancient masters."
>
> Hearing him respond this way, I suddenly felt ashamed and surprised, so I asked him, "What are words? What is practice?"

The tenzo said, "If you penetrate this question, how can you fail to become a person of understanding?"*

Sometimes the last sentence is translated: "If you hold this question close to your heart, you cannot fail to become a person of understanding."

Here Zen Master Dōgen asks the question that we continue to ask ourselves about kitchen work: "Is there anything good about it?" Don't we have more important things to do? Doing important work that benefits others, or simply earning a living, or perhaps attaining fame and fortune (possibly even as a spiritual person meditating and studying), enjoying ourselves—perhaps skiing, hang gliding or rock climbing—or properly relaxing and being entertained? I'm still sorting out how to spend my time here on planet Earth. Shouldn't there be something to show for my time here?

To understand the answer to this inquiry, the cook-monk attests that we will need to keep the question close to our heart and see what we can find out. We'll need to sacrifice some of the other possibilities, show up in the kitchen, and do something with our blood, sweat, and tears. Do something with devotion. In our world, devotion to a noble cause is exalted, while devotion to working in the kitchen is seen as somehow misguided. It certainly doesn't pay well. And now eighty-eight billionaires have as much wealth as the rest of the population. They are clearly devoted. *To what?* we might wonder, *aside from making more money?*

While we appreciate sacrifices being made for physical adventures, we don't always understand the "tea and rice (effort) of daily activity." A whole pot of beet soup floods the floor. Nuts burn. We have no food left inside, so we must let the food

*from *Moon in a Dewdrop* translated by Kazauki Tanahashi

speak for itself. We absorb the pain, grow larger-hearted, clean up the mess, and carry on. "To heal," said Stephen Levine, "is to touch with love that which we previously touched with fear." What good work.

In a fascinating article in the *New Yorker*, Japanese Zen priest Ittetsu Nemoto describes how he was about to drop a giant pot when huge energy washed through him. He could do anything. In a similar fashion, the poet Rumi encourages us to meet this "clear consciousness core of your being, the same in ecstasy as in self-hating fatigue."

We may be impressed by the dedication of professional athletes aiming for peak performance, while facing the everyday tumult leaves us cold. The saying in Zen is that we are like rocks in a tumbler. Getting the rough edges knocked off, we emerge smooth and polished. Unfortunately for our self-esteem, while being tossed and turned, we probably have not developed any muscles with which to flex and impress.

The Black Dragon Jewel

Through one word, or seven words, or three times five,
even if you thoroughly investigate myriad forms,
nothing can be depended upon.
Night advances, the moon glows and falls into the ocean.
The black dragon jewel you have been searching for is everywhere.

XUEDOU (J. SETCHŌ)

Tracing Dōgen's story, we find in *Tenzo Kyōkun* that he has the good fortune to meet the tenzo-monk from the ship again. Here is his account:

> I was moved with joy. I served him tea, and we talked. When I referred to the discussion of words and practice, which had taken place on the ship, the tenzo said, "To study words you must know the origin of words. To endeavor in practice you must know the origin of practice."
>
> I asked, "What are words?"
>
> The tenzo said, "One, two, three, four, five."
>
> I asked again, "What is practice?"
>
> "Nothing in the entire universe is hidden."
>
> We talked about many other things, which I will not introduce now. If I know a little about words or understand practice, it is because of the great help of the tenzo. I told my late master Myosin about this in detail, and he was extremely pleased.

I later found a verse which Xuedou—(known as Setchō in Japanese, a highly venerated monk in twelfth-century China)—wrote for a monk:

> Through one word, or seven words, or three times five,
> even if you thoroughly investigate myriad forms,
> nothing can be depended upon.
> Night advances, the moon glows and falls into
>   the ocean.
> The black dragon jewel you have been searching
>   for is everywhere.

What the tenzo had told me corresponded with Xuedou's poem. So I knew all the more that the tenzo was truly a person of the way.

The black dragon jewel that you have been searching for is everywhere. When I first heard this, it went straight inside to a place that responded, *Oh, of course,* followed by an immediate softening and receiving. Love, what is precious, what is healing, is everywhere, when you hold the moment close and are willing to receive the comfort and love that is available.

Nothing in the entire universe is hidden means (among other things) that it's no secret that money and accomplishments may not bring you love or the feeling of preciousness inside that you have been searching for. It's no secret that when you focus on one thing, everything is included. What you've been searching for is everywhere—and does not depend on your performance but on your willingness to receive the treasure that cannot be earned.

In the kitchen or out, when you give your heart to something, you feel your heart. When you let things come home to your heart, you feel the love from Beyond. Cooking may or may not be a place for you to find this out. You'll have to see.

A Student Asks, "Why Haven't You Enlightened Me Yet?"

When a student at Tassajara asked Suzuki Roshi, "Why haven't you enlightened me yet?" his response was, "I'm making my best effort." I found that a phenomenal expression of love, of not being hooked by the student's thinking. The question seemed disrespectful, as well as ill considered. Whose work is it after all, your enlightenment? In fact, we could say that everything is making its best effort to enlighten you—*the black dragon jewel is everywhere*. And so, who is not letting enlightenment occur?

Which brings us back to Dōgen and his question about kitchen work in the *Tenzo Kyōkun*, "Is there anything good about it?" The answer is not to be found in the standards of the world—perhaps money, power, rank, fame—which never quite suffice, but in you yourself. You lighten up. You let what is Beyond flow into you, flow through you. You offer your heart and your hands, your awareness to bringing forth food.

11

DOING THE WORK
YOURSELF

To enter the kitchen and prepare food necessitates
working and could possibly arouse intense emotion—
that is to say, cook's temperament. You may find either
or both formidable, formidable enough that you wish
to back out or call for reinforcements. Perhaps you set
out to demonstrate your worth by cooking, and now
you are the one getting cooked, stewed or skewered,
sweaty and steamed. Just as the ingredients need to be
made presentable—cooking, seasoning, assembly, and
structure all have their place—the cook may also require
transformation of awareness. Often the learning curve is
so steep that cooks end up back in front of the television
with take-out in hand. If you decide to persevere in your
endeavor to cook, you will need to come to standing,
regroup and refocus, show up, and do the one next thing.

Reinhabiting Your Body:
You Are the Secret Ingredient

*What is ordinary is that people seek for what is extraordinary,
while what is extraordinary is when people settle down
in the ordinary and bring it to life.*

SUZUKI ROSHI

I remember watching people at Tassajara when I cooked there in the sixties and marveling at how often they did not know how to sweep the floor. A broom? What is that? I would guess it's only gotten worse. And how do you use your hands to wash dishes? Or to cut vegetables? We're becoming all thumbs—in more ways than texting.

One tradition of spiritual practice seems to emphasize becoming well versed in transcendence. You rise above. You become detached. You work to remain up there, not letting things bring you down. Often this goes along with a rejection of the material world—after all, you're above that stuff. Relating with the material world sometimes becomes more and more impossible. After all, while you were up and out, things on the earth plane did not receive the attention they need to function smoothly, so when you do come down, difficulties or disorder may confront you—sometimes in your own body.

On the other hand, Zen focuses on immanence: the spiritual is right here, right now. The emphasis is on reinhabiting your own body. *You* move back in—that is, you devote more of your awareness to receiving sensations from your body and spend less time ignoring your body or giving your body directives from the head. Rather than being *up* and *out*, you find yourself *here*. As the poet Kabir puts it: "Enter into your own body. There you'll find a solid place to put your feet. Think about it carefully. Don't go off somewhere else."

Most commonly moving back into our bodies necessitates undertaking some specifics: we sit, dig, work at a task; we do a downward dog; we bow, we meditate, or we cook, cut, chop, clean. Though exercise can be exhilarating, we often overlook or override the information coming from the body and focus on performance. So to overcome or reverse a lifetime of habits and become more intimately acquainted with the body—that is, embodied—we usually need to be doing specific things, whether they are forms, practices, or activities. Cooking, gardening, yoga, theater, dance, meditation—you find yourself here manifesting. Your movements, your very stance is less oriented to posturing and becomes more aligned with your essence. We call that authenticity: sending your roots down into the ground, growing tall inside.

While teaching cooking classes for many years now, I have noticed a great diversity in how people work. Where is their attention? Often it goes into conversation, and when it goes into voicing words, their attention is not connecting with their bodies and what their hands could be doing—if they were not busy speaking.

My sense is that we do not have much understanding of the value of work here in the West. When, for instance, I worked at the post office as a Christmastime temp, most people seemed to revel in doing as little as they could and still get paid: long breaks, sluggish movements, and criticism of anybody working. "Slow down," they'd say, "you're making us look bad." My apologies, but I enjoyed being focused and energized and just didn't know how to put my mind somewhere else where it would not be engaged in what was right in front of me. Much of our attention is simply being lost in the trance of everyday reality, the perpetual sleep of an unexamined life.

I did chores growing up, and I took to the work quite naturally. We were family, and each of us was to do our part. Of course, I wanted to get finished so that I could play, but I also wanted to do a fine job. Weekly I cleaned the family bathroom. I don't remember anyone showing me how to do this. I used a sponge to scrub with cleanser, then rinsed with warm water, and finally with the sponge cleanly wrung out, wiped up the rinsing. I still recall how the white enamel sparkled, and stainless steel gleamed. No, this is not an advertisement for a product, but a word for work. You are the secret ingredient: your heart connecting with your hands and the objects of the world.

And as you reinhabit your body, you become more awake and alive—your hands for one become hands. Finding your hands, you may discover that they love doing things—that's what they are for! Opposable thumbs make us human (opposable means that there are also fingers at work). When it comes to work, think about it: Who is it who would rather not work, you or your hands? We think of freedom as not having to do things with our hands, yet a greater freedom is being able to use our hands to do things, rather than handcuffing ourselves with wishful thinking about doing as little as possible. What freedom do you have in handcuffs?

Zen Master Dōgen Marvels:
A Mushroom Story

*Realizing the mystery is nothing but breaking through
to grasp an ordinary person's life.*
ZEN MASTER DESHAN

Even Zen Master Dōgen had his doubts about the value of working in the kitchen. On his pilgrimage to China from Japan in the early thirteenth century, he sought to clarify the great matter of life and death—if we have spiritual nature, why do we need to practice manifesting it? During this time, he met his teacher Juching, who affirmed Dōgen's practice-realization. Also while in China, he met two tenzos, the cook-monks, who impressed him deeply. One meeting I described earlier; here now is how Dōgen describes meeting the other cook-monk, who was . . .

in front of the Buddha hall drying some mushrooms in the sun. He had a bamboo stick in his hand and no hat on his head. The sun was very hot, scorching the pavement. It looked very painful; his backbone was bent like a bow, and his eyebrows were as white as a crane.

I went up to the tenzo and asked, "How long have you been a monk?"

"Sixty-eight years," he replied.

"Why don't you let a helper do it?"

"Others are not myself."

"Reverend Sir, you follow regulations exactly, but as the sun is so hot, why do you work so hard as this?"

"Until when should I wait?"

So I stopped talking. As I was walking farther along the covered walkway, I thought about how important the tenzo's position is.

How striking it is when someone exemplifies this spirit, taking on a challenging task—and some days most any task qualifies as challenging—with steadfast commitment: *Why not have someone else do it? They are not me.* And then seeing it through with minimum hesitation on the spot: *As the sun is so hot, why don't you do it at another time? That would not be now.*

We often venerate this attitude in our professional sports heroes, perhaps paying them excessively and often forgiving them their misconduct. They are seen as having extraordinary talents and accomplishments, and perhaps they help our team win. Yet is that the point? Should you not cook if you cannot be the best of the best and produce masterpiece after masterpiece? Should you not cook if you cannot sell it at a profit?

"What is extraordinary," says Suzuki Roshi, "is to settle down in the ordinary and bring it alive." To cook and to clean, to plant and to harvest. To see the virtue of this effort means shifting your focus away from peak performance and tuning in to the rhythms of your body on the spot as you go about your day. And far beyond the applause, we can appreciate our sincere and wholehearted efforts to benefit our families and ourselves—especially when our children are small.

As my daughter said sometime during her daughter's first year, "Dad, why doesn't anyone tell you how hard it is?" And we can't possibly say, as in the midst of it, we are inoculated with love. "Dad," she had attested months earlier, "I had no idea it was possible to love someone so much." Everything becomes the world of our baby, and we labor with care and feeding, tears and trials. It's extraordinary. It's an initiation that you have to undergo for yourself—all the fatigue and rawness—with your whole body and mind. Then you know for yourself. And you still cannot tell others. Words cannot convey it.

And cooking, if you choose to do it, can be like this—with no stopping to assess if it makes any sense or is worth your while. It's not an investment where you check on your rate of return, but an offering you make to yourself and others because you want to be that generous—and no one, as the mushroom-drying cook remarks, can take your place.

<hr />

At Home, at Work, in Your Body

Listen what I have to say, when you get that good advice.
Don't let it waste away. Take it from me. I know.
Undeveloped mind don't mean a thing.
We've got to wake up, baby.
Nothing come to sleepers but a dream.
LOWELL FULSOM, FROM HIS SONG "SLEEPER"

Working itself can be a way to practice entering your body. How are you doing what you do? Do you have feet? Are they on the floor? Relationship and the possibilities for connection are everywhere. Whether you've studied this in walking meditation, you can study it in the kitchen: sense your feet and legs receiving the support of the earth rather than pushing it away. This support is associated with ease—you're feeling at home in your body in the kitchen, this place of cooking. And it is associated with coming to your senses rather than telling them what they have to be doing. You're receiving information rather than dispensing directives. (Dispensing directives can be all the more useful as it accords with the information you've received.)

You can visualize sending roots down that bring up resources to nourish you. You're coming to standing rather than abandoning your body in a standing position, while you focus on mental issues or the work at hand. Ease comes from efforting less as you allow your body to come into alignment with the energetics of standing. Not something for me to tell you how but something for you to study, to notice, to practice.

Seeing with your eyes and working with your hands is also feeling your way along in the dark. What is going on? How will you work with it? Attention, focus, energy, concentration. Letting things come and abide in your heart. Letting your heart return and abide in things. You study what needs to happen to make food and how to make that happen. Perceive and observe.

Implicitly this means being willing to try out movements, especially of your hands, which you may never have tried before. Just because a movement is unfamiliar does not mean that it is awkward. Some movements that are initially unfamiliar turn out to embody true ease. Cutting is like this: sawing as well as chopping with the knife makes cutting easier than chopping only. To find this out, practice sawing while you cut, and feel what your hands are feeling: *easy* does it. When I visited the New England Culinary Institute many years ago, one of the teachers mentioned that almost every new student needed to learn this: rocking the knife forward and backward and not simply up and down.

I think of this as basic Buddhism: experience your experience more closely. No, not in terms of making it more to your liking or more acceptable but to observe more intently and carefully: everything is there, and what will you make of it? Perhaps you bring some aspects forward and allow others to recede into the background.

12

FOOD CHOICES

Cooks nowadays have a great choice of ingredients, brought
about by affluence: oil, transportation, refrigeration. And,
of course, huge segments of our economy profit from
turning food into products. Wouldn't buying in save
you time and effort? Faced with boundless information
presented as scientific truth and ethical stands promoting
the sanctity of life, a cook may believe that eating wisely
means following the expert of your choosing and obeying
what they say. Yet this would be abandoning your own
capacity for sensing, tasting, discovering what works
best for you, and that may not be wise. Receiving the
ingredients with gratitude, observing your experience
closely, you find your way.

Choosing Food

In the early thirteenth century, Zen Master Dōgen advised: "When preparing the vegetables and the soup ingredients to be cooked, do not discuss the quantity or quality of these materials which have been obtained from the monastery officers; just prepare them with sincerity. Most of all you should avoid getting upset or complaining about the quantity of the food materials."

When you read Dōgen's advice about how to handle food, you quickly realize that today we live in an inconceivably different world—one of affluence. My local supermarket has local butter, organic butter, butter from grass-fed cows, from Ireland, from Devon, "European-style" butter from the American Midwest. "Do not discuss the quantity or quality of these materials." Are you kidding? Now we are beset with an astonishing number of choices to make. As Michael Pollan brilliantly points out, it's *The Omnivore's Dilemma*: what to eat, which choices to make.

Over the centuries, Buddhists were much closer to Zen Master Dōgen. Originally, those ordained into the Buddhist order were to go begging for food each day and to eat only before noon. You were to eat what you received—so monks were not necessarily vegetarian, as not everyone offering food was vegetarian. And those offering food did not provide menus, nor were the monks allowed to specify their food preferences.

Today, curiously enough, I've heard that monks in Southeast Asia are frequently beset with large portions of meat, as these offerings are considered worthy of greater merit (accruing to those making the offerings).

Once practitioners began to gather into monasteries, most commonly they chose to be vegetarian, in accord with the basic Buddhist dictum "not to harm." The most obvious exception was Tibet, where vegetarians were rare, and most everyone, including monks, ate meat. To my knowledge, the practice of eating meat among Tibetans and students of Tibetan Buddhism has often continued when they relocate outside of Tibet.

Following in the Japanese Zen tradition, we were instructed to "eat what you are served." So when we were at the center, we were vegetarian; if we were eating at someone's home, we followed the customs of the house; and if we were dining out at a restaurant, we were allowed to order off the menu as we chose.

Another guideline we were given was the traditional admonition not to eat meat that was specifically killed for you. This, as might be suspected, has become gnarly, which is to say that some Buddhists ask a go-between (the non-Buddhists) to have meat killed for them and then to sell it to the Buddhists (not that they wanted any killing done on their behalf). Also, more than one modern-day Buddhist, thinking this through rather carefully, has concluded that the most ethical conduct is to eat meat *only* if you have killed it yourself.

Suzuki Roshi was on the whole very patient with us, yet at various times he also expressed his dislike for "food trips." One, perhaps amusing, story about Roshi happened when he was on a town trip from Tassajara with a student who had become a righteous vegetarian. Tassajara is, of course, at the end of a fourteen-mile-long dirt road that climbs and descends three thousand feet—the nearest town is about two hours away.

When Roshi suggested that they stop for lunch, the student started looking for a place with vegetarian food. Before he spotted anything, Roshi said, "Let's eat there," pointing to a diner. So the student agreed, and after entering the diner, they sat down in a booth. Embarking on a concerned search of the menu, the student was relieved to find that he could order a grilled-cheese sandwich. Roshi ordered a hamburger, "double meat."

When their food came, and they had each taken a bite, Roshi asked, "How's your food?" After the student responded, "Good, good," Roshi commented, "I don't like mine. Let's switch." He proceeded to shift the plates, so that the student could only stare dumbfounded, and then, being devoted to his teacher, the student proceeded to eat the burger.

Nowadays I doubt that any American Zen teacher could get away with this: "Out of line! Outrageous!" It's holy and spiritual to be vegetarian, the right thing to do. And it's not up to your Zen teacher to bust your righteousness, but to be complicit.

What's worth noting is that Suzuki Roshi didn't mind if you were a vegetarian or a meat-eater. At issue was someone saying that we should all be vegetarian. It's not always so. It's one thing to know for yourself what you choose to do and another to attempt to impose the *right* way, your way, on everyone. You're acting from your head, from the realm of thinking, rather than experiencing food closely enough to be able to make what are wise choices for you. And you are implying that others are incapable of making their own clear discernments, so you need to tell them what to do.

Frequently we do not trust our choices, or we worry that others will challenge them. We look to reason or to those we believe are right-thinking to back up the choices we've made. And soon enough we are living in that world, the world of consensus, not the world of our experiencing carefully and knowing for ourselves. Consensus means that we are no longer making choices for ourselves. We're buying what's on the shelves.

For instance, two of my friends who are diabetic never (or rarely) take insulin. They eat primarily meat and vegetables, even eliminating those vegetables—carrots and onions among them—that are high in carbohydrates. They prize nuts, especially macadamia, and decline fruits for their high sugar content. People have found that not taking insulin is a huge health benefit for those with diabetes. As someone who has consumed huge quantities of carbohydrates for about forty years as primarily a vegetarian, I'm headed in that direction as well: my latest test results show fasting blood sugar levels in the prediabetic range.

A different example of Roshi's attitude was exhibited in his response to a student who was eating only what was served in the third bowl, rather than the first two bowls as well. In our meals in the meditation hall, we usually eat from a set of three bowls, and the third, or smallest one, was the one most likely to be a salad, vegetables, or fruit, rather than grains or beans. Others kept telling this student that "our practice is to accept some food in each bowl." After listening to students complain that one person was not "practicing our way," Roshi called the student in for a visit and asked what he was doing at meals in the zendo. "I'm trying to find out how I feel if I eat only the food in the third bowl." Roshi congratulated him, "Oh, good! You should always be finding out how things work." And that was that. If the student had said he was avoiding carbohydrates (because they were bad for you), Roshi might well have had a different response.

The last time I saw this friend (who told me this story), he had been eating only raw food for ten years, and though staying at my house, he would not let me not cook for him—that is, prepare raw foods for him. He meticulously prepared all his own meals.

When it comes to eating, we frequently have things backward. We put a high value on obedience, while putting little value on permission and empowerment. Instead of following our nose to choose our food, we follow the culture's latest food trends or what someone somewhere says is best, the one, the only way to eat. Or we frequent fast-food franchises and eat food designed to push all the right flavor buttons.

Sometimes we are swayed by what the counter-culture proclaims: vegetarian, vegan, Buddhist, Zen. In any case, when we more or less blindly follow along, we are abandoning our own capacity to find out for ourselves, neglecting to use our own interest and curiosity, our beginner's mind. And, of course, often we are following our unexamined impulses, reaching out for what's easy.

The implicit assumption we often make is that we could never figure out anything for ourselves—that is, something that would be well beyond question or reproach—so we better do what those who really know tell us. Although that is sometimes called eating wisely, how wise is it to abandon your capacity to find out? Do they know you as you know you? How could they possibly have a formula that matches your uniqueness, your capacity to taste and experience, to explore and play, to enjoy and savor? This does not mean you cannot try out what they propose and see for yourself if it makes sense to you.

To eat is to take in life and make it yours—to make the world you. Permission is simply to allow, to permit yourself to live life, to taste, to try things out. Empowerment is knowing from your own experience. If you want to do it by the book, okay, but if you want to do it from your heart, from your felt sense, give yourself back your capacity to make your own choices rather than doing what the world tells you.

Finding Out for Yourself

Obeying what the world tells you to do is often limited in terms of beneficial results. Diets are notorious for helping people lose a lot of weight only to gain back even more. The good news is that deciding to figure it out for yourself is one of the most powerful decisions you will ever make in your life.

Years after the fact, I found out that one of my dear friends at the San Francisco Zen Center had been bulimic. Books were not the answer, and her psychologist *fired* her for "having too much resistance," and the guru couldn't be trusted. Finally, she came to realize that if anyone was going to figure out what to do, it would have to be her. So she decided to find out for herself even though, she says, she had absolutely no reason to believe that she could—because she never had. These decisions often embody great transformative power, as do the epiphanies of those hitting bottom and deciding to become sober.

To find out for herself what to do, she realized she would need to study her experience more closely, to discover what was actually going on. Her effort was to remain conscious, observing as clearly and carefully as possible what was happening moment after moment. One aspect of her method was to keep notebooks about her eating, tracking as much as she could, whether she was binging or not.

It didn't matter whether she was doing the right thing; what was important to her was to be aware, to be conscious of what was happening. Of course, the writing helped because she had to make mental notes of what was going on to get them down on paper.

Little by little, during that time, she began noticing sensations, feelings, and thoughts, including anger and sexual desire, which she had not wanted to acknowledge. Such a profound shift, from instituting a picture of what life by decree must look like inside, to allowing the inner world to surface with its own truths. The inner judge, who previously had conspired to find ways to keep her feelings stuffed, was enlisted now as a more and more impartial observer. *What do you notice? Help me write it down.* It took her about four years, she said, to be thoroughly over the bulimia. Yet the most important thing had been her decision to find out for herself what was going on and what to do about it and to renew that decision again and again.

You decide. When you confirm that it's up to you, blessings will come home to your heart.

Observing What to Eat

After about forty years of following primarily a vegetarian diet, I began eating meat several years ago. Of course, I'm not saying that everyone should eat meat, but I'd like to explain how I came to it, through my experience. While never really considering myself a vegetarian, I ate most of my meals at the Zen Center for twenty years, where we followed a vegetarian diet. While I was there, eggs and dairy were often included. Later, their diet was frequently vegan. Since I do not visit often now, I don't know what the Center's current diet is.

What I noticed during all my years at the Zen Center was that on a vegetarian diet, with less than adequate sleep, I consistently craved the next fix of caffeine and sugar. Where are the cookies? Where is the coffee? Is it time for a break?

But, of course, even the *fixes* did not work. I would have enough coffee that after the sixth or seventh cup I could go right to sleep. You can only kick your horse with caffeine so much and then you crash. I would eat sugar, and the energetic hit was so dazzling I'd keep having more—great!—until the insulin would kick in to lower my sugar levels and I'd find myself with the sugar blues.

I could rationalize that I was doing the right thing, not killing animals, yet in reality, I was drooping through my life, propped up by a focused will and a strong drive to perform and fit in. And that became more and more difficult for me through my forties, fifties, and sixties. Back out in the world, I finally realized that my diet was no longer sustaining me and acknowledged that it never had. I had survived with youthful drive and determination, and I was no longer youthful.

So I began eating meat, starting with some grass-fed ground beef. I'm fortunate to live in an area with many resources for high-quality meats. I added salt and pepper and shaped some meatballs, fried them briefly, adding some sherry at the finish, and set them aside. Then I stir-fried some vegetables with garlic and ginger, before adding back the meatballs. The meat with all of its oils tasted so delicious and felt so vitalizing. Soon my energy stabilized, and I stopped looking for my next snack.

Scott Blossom, a friend of mine who is also an acupuncturist and yoga teacher with knowledge about Ayurveda, explained to me that when your body has enough fat, it sends a signal to your brain that you've had enough. With sugar and carbohydrates, however, no messages are forthcoming. Any excess of carbohydrates or sugar is stored in your body as fat. When eating carbohydrates, the signal to your brain is much slower because your blood sugar level has to register in the brain. This can take perhaps half an hour, while you continue to eat. Though full, you're likely to keep eating, until finally the signal arrives.

For years our culture has been demonizing fat and red meat while putting high-fructose corn syrup into everything—even the turkey in my turkey sandwich on United Airlines had corn syrup. My partner and I notice these things because Margot cannot tolerate any corn or corn derivatives—so basically she cannot eat food "product" because corn derivatives of some sort are in most of them.

Whenever I would eat a packaged snack, I would feel full—that is, more or less bloated—and at the same time hungry. Noticing this over and over, I began to wonder why I would do that to myself. Again, once I began eating some meat, my energy stabilized, and I was no longer looking for the next quick food fix.

⟶

Cons and Myths

About 2005, my friend Layna Berman introduced me to both *The Great Cholesterol Con* by Dr. Malcolm Kendrick and *The Vegetarian Myth* by Lierre Keith. Layna has been a student of health and fitness for most of her life. Along with her partner, Jeffrey Fawcett, they have a website, yourownhealthandfitness. org, that offers "a critical, independent voice" on health matters. I found the books fairly illuminating; they corroborated much of what I had been experiencing in my own diet.

For years I had been telling my doctors that I wouldn't take statin drugs and risk damaging my liver to promote supposed heart health. "Don't you understand? My liver has enough problems as it is, without having to work harder to produce more cholesterol because the statin drugs have removed it from circulation—our bodies need cholesterol." An acupuncturist once told me that I had "constrained liver qi." Really? "Yes, Ed, with women it's called PMS, but that's only a few days a month. You have it all the time." And someone is suggesting that I ask my liver to work harder to make up for the cholesterol missing from circulation? I think not.

The side effects of statin drugs are not commonly attributed to the statins. I am not a doctor, not an expert. I do, however, have two friends who have had dreadful health issues (peripheral neuropathy and depression to the point of attempted suicide) that in my view can readily be attributed to statin drugs. Just my word here—and two billion dollars a year in sales say that I am wrong. If you are interested, read the book and make your own decisions.

Dr. Kendrick, who started out believing the cholesterol con, has concluded that the evidence for cholesterol causing heart disease "is [   ]"—the blank space in brackets, he explains, is there just in case they ever find any evidence for this! Instead, his conclusion is that heart disease is caused by stress. Curiously, this research goes back to the seventies (when the correlation was made between stress and type-A behavior), but you don't make a financial killing counseling people about altering their type-A behavior. Still, reducing stress has been shown to dramatically reduce the risk of heart disease. Apparently, one study in which all participants had the same diet, support groups, exercise, and so forth was discontinued when too many of the people not receiving the counseling for type-A behavior were dying of heart attacks. After more than thirty-five years of serious Buddhist meditation practice, even I needed counseling to reduce my type-A behavior!

Type-A personalities keep trying to do more—sometimes way more—than they possibly can. In my case, it meant being frustrated and angry when people or things slowed me down and got in my way, and being anxious, worried, depressed, and despondent when I couldn't accomplish everything on my list. I was simply trying to do too much. "You can't do it," my psychiatrist would say, "even for one day."

I had to focus on making the instructed changes, and what a world of difference it made! Most of my emotional volatility cleared up. Type-A behavior is not nutritionally based and does not require medication. I needed help to correctly identify the problem and then put in place new behaviors. I feel fortunate to have received the help that I did, because generally our world these days seeks to get you on meds. Three simple guidelines I now use: work only on designated projects or for particular periods of time; take a break and do something enjoyable; do not think about anything you have to do after midnight tonight.

Is fat the problem? Or sugar? After all, any excess sugar we eat is stored in our bodies as fat, which alters our metabolism, and all carbohydrates break down into sugar. If you are curious about this, you can Google these articles by Gary Taubes, which appeared in the *New York Times Magazine*: "What If It's All Been a Big Fat Lie?" (2002) and "Is Sugar Toxic?" (2011). His books, such as *Why We Get Fat*, are also helpful. I'll leave it to you to study if you wish. Even in the world of science, this is controversial, so you will need to decide for yourself.

Taubes's writing confirmed what I was experiencing: my high carbohydrate intake was consistently leaving me lethargic, and when I reduced my carbohydrates and started to eat meat, I began having solid, lasting energy and stopped looking for the next cookie, cracker, candy, and caffeine fix. Eating some meat combined with greatly reduced carbohydrates and generous portions of vegetables was pivotal to my greater well-being. If you undertake your own study, you can find out what works for you.

Another secret that others seemed to know, though I did not, is that tofu has high quantities of estrogen-precursors. When I was largely vegetarian, I ate tofu several times a week. With some prompting, I finally had a saliva test for estrogen levels, and they turned out to be double what is normal for a male my age. When a man has estrogen levels this high, I can assure you he is not happy: mood swings, depression, trouble sleeping. I had ten of the eleven symptoms—I was spared "weight gain around the hips." Six months after I stopped eating tofu, I took the test again, and my estrogen levels were normal: happy man. Sometimes reading, study, or advice can give us a healthy new direction.

Lierre Keith's *The Vegetarian Myth* is a wonderfully thoughtful book about diet and lifestyle. While reminding readers that she is not trying to tell them what to do but encouraging them to make dietary decisions for themselves, she encourages us to look carefully. An important piece of her background is that she was a practicing vegan for about twenty years.

One of her poignant reminders is that to grow plants, agriculture destroys the habitat that previously provided a home for many creatures. Not only is habitat destroyed but also topsoil. Much of the topsoil that was once in the American Midwest is now gone; of the two or three feet of topsoil that once covered the plains, only inches remain! It's not the kind of killing that we can readily see, as we do with the killing of cows, chickens, or pigs. This killing is largely unspoken.

Without topsoil, farming is difficult. Ms. Keith also points out that we need to feed the soil, which historically was often done with animal waste. Nowadays, we commonly feed the soil with oil that has been transformed into fertilizer through the use of more oil. Procuring oil is often not seen as involving any killing or wars or devastation of land. Yet when we acknowledge that the use of oil comes at a cost, we see that suffering in various forms is deeply intertwined in food production, whether or not meat is being eaten.

Some inspiring news in all of this is the work being done by Joel Salatin and his family at Polyface Farms in the Shenandoah Valley of Virginia. Polyface Farms offers a truly exceptional story of restoring topsoil as well as providing an abundance of produce. They do this by moving their cows to a new pasture each day, altering the fences so that the grasses remain close to full-grown with a healthy root structure that prevents erosion. They also use portable chicken houses, on wheels, that are brought in three days later. The chickens come racing out of their roosts to gobble up the maggots in the cow pies, which breaks up the pies for fertilizing the soil. The topsoil has been building up, so that now a fence post can be driven into the earth in places that had been rock.

All in all, there are deep and fundamental questions buried in the American way of life. How will we treat people, animals, and the land so that we can prosper and live in harmony with the earth and all beings? It's possible that the quest for short-term profits (affluence) does not account for all the hidden long-term costs. Time will tell—only by that time, there may be no telling. For telling, someone needs to be listening.

13

EATING

Eating perpetuates our lifeblood. Food comes from far away, from the work of countless people and from the working of other forms of life, both plants and animals—a gift from Creation. To give thanks is an act of honoring the sanctity of life and the incredible effort that goes into life giving life to life. To enjoy our food is likewise a way of honoring the ingredients that come to us, bringing them to life through our awareness while we are eating.

To enjoy food is often a hard-earned fruit, not the same as greed or lust, which in a rush of excitement or frenzy focuses on making food disappear. Little is observed about the food in such a rush, only that it gets us off, getting us high or reliably taking us down, beyond any inner turmoil. On the other hand, enjoyment, which is our capacity to resonate with the objects of our awareness, offers us relief from misguided efforts to avoid the sensory world and our inner demons. We can experience wholesome connection and feel at home in the world. With the attention and discipline of enjoying our food, we tend to make wise choices about what we eat and how much. We develop skills for living in this world rather than trying to avoid it.

Not What to Eat, But How

We venerate the three treasures
and give thanks for this food:
the work of many people,
the offering of other forms of life.
May this food nourish us,
body, mind, and spirit.
May all beings be happy,
healthy, and free from suffering.

MEAL PRAYER

Do not complain about the quality or quantity of the food offered.

ZEN MASTER DŌGEN

Zen practice traditionally has put much more emphasis on *how* we eat rather than *what* we eat. Cultures of affluence, where a plethora of choices is available, are for the most part rather recent in human history. John Blofeld in his autobiographical *The Wheel of Life* describes practicing at a Zen monastery in China—in the early 1930s as I recall—where the three meals were largely rice (with weevils) in the first bowl, broth from cooking pumpkin in the second bowl, the stewed pumpkin itself in the third bowl. Occasionally benefiting from the generosity of donors, they would have a feast of vegetables cooked in *oil*. With Mr. Blofeld's setting the word *oil* in italics, you can feel his tears of joy. While he laments not being more committed, I am in awe of his enduring this practice for several months!

Zen practice in the West is no longer impoverished in that way. While Buddhism in the East is known as "the Middle Way," here it has been transformed into "the *Upper* Middle Way," with various food agendas competing for attention: Is it organic? vegetarian? vegan? pure enough? ethical enough? And food allergies or sensitivities are almost impossible to enumerate and certainly not to reconcile: issues with dairy, wheat, soy, corn, and nuts are common enough, but out of forty or fifty people, you can be expected to add garlic, beets, green peppers, red peppers, onion, eggs, and a few other miscellaneous foods that challenge someone's digestive system—and we cannot afford to be dismissive because sometimes the consequences of eating the wrong food can be dire, possibly requiring hospitalization. So, in many cases, more than simply liking or disliking a food is at stake.

When Buddhist monks went out begging for their food or lived together in monasteries, the practice of eating meant learning to tolerate pleasant and unpleasant foods, and taking in food was a metaphor for taking in life, receiving and digesting innumerable moments of experience that will be delicious or unappetizing. The practice of eating teaches us to chew, swallow, and digest what comes into our body and into our world, understanding that much of what comes our way is beyond our control and recognizing that how we control things may not be in our best interest. While making conscious choices, informed by information and personal experience, is pivotal to our well-being, we may also find that when we exercise our choice, we become caught in a web of successes and failures, happiness and disappointment, depending on how well we are doing at getting our way. We may also find that our narrow range of choices makes it problematic to tolerate the wider range of what life brings our way. So instead of picking and choosing, as students of life we might at times choose to practice acceptance, gratitude, enjoyment, thanksgiving. We can not only practice tasting and eating but also study the *nature* of tasting and eating.

The Ceremony of Eating

Having practiced Zen in simpler times, I was able to avoid many food battles and focus on how to eat rather than on what to eat. Without any opportunity for choosing, we practiced bowing and receiving the food that was put into our bowls.

There's some irony to this because during training times, meals take place in the meditation hall and involve specific formalities. Although these meals often take forty-five to fifty minutes, only about seven or perhaps eight minutes are devoted to actually eating. Each meal is a ceremony in and of itself, beginning with placing a food offering on the altar, which is accompanied by a crescendo of drumming. A meal chant commences, with the clacking of two wooden sticks. An oryoki, a set of nested eating bowls, is carefully opened from its cloth wrapping and positioned just so in front of our knees (all this time we are sitting cross-legged), along with the chopsticks, spoon, lap napkin, cleaning stick, and drying cloth.

Further chanting leads to the serving of food. Each server bows to a pair of students, who bow in return, and the food is portioned out, followed by another mutual bow—and the servers proceed down the row. When the serving is complete, renewed chanting leads to eating. The largest bowl of food is held aloft in veneration, and at last, we have permission to begin ingesting food. We eat in silence. The meal concludes with the washing and drying of our dishes, along with the repacking and rewrapping of the oryoki. Seven minutes of actual eating time is rather brief, so each of us needs to focus on the business of getting our food chewed and swallowed in the time allotted.

While many Westerners are reluctant participants in ceremony, there is at the same time little understanding of where the absence of ceremony leaves us. Many years ago, I participated in a workshop on eating orders and disorders with a Lacanian psychologist named André Patsalides. One thing Dr. Patsalides pointed out, based on well-documented evidence, is that cultures with extensive ceremony around food have fewer eating disorders, while cultures lacking ceremony around eating have more eating disorders. This seems to apply to the United States: scant ceremony and a beautiful range of disorders, including obesity, bulimia, and anorexia. In other words, eating is often a profane activity, whereas the creation of sacred space for eating requires attention, suitable structure, and prayer.

Meanwhile the scant ceremony remaining continues to disappear. Apparently the sales of breakfast cereals—add milk (dairy or nondairy), sugar, and perhaps sliced banana—have plummeted significantly. People do not want to have to wash the bowl! It's too much effort without reward. From a Zen perspective, it's shortsighted. To paraphrase a passage from Zen Master Dōgen, "Because you were looking somewhere else, you did not notice that washing your bowl is realization." Ceremony means you just do it as a practice, regardless of your assessment of its worth—and perhaps you will find yourself entering the moment as deeply as you are able.

One well-known Zen story concerns a monk asking the famous Zen master Joshu for instruction: "I have just entered the monastery. Please instruct me." So Joshu asks him, "Have you eaten your breakfast?" When the monk replies, "Yes, I have eaten," Joshu responds, "Then go wash your bowls." Can't be bothered? Then skip it and let what is loudest or most insistent (inside or out) grab your attention, as you allow yourself to be swept along with this attention-demanding flow. It's incessant, and sometimes you may find it burdensome—you're so much at the mercy of the waves. Still, when you pause, you realize that you have choice.

Under what circumstances do we eat—that is, what, if any, ceremony prevails? Is it sitting or standing, walking down the street, in the car while driving? While watching television? At a meal with others, and if so, is it stressful or enjoyable? Is there a meal prayer? The saying of grace? Do we offer thanks, gratitude, blessings? Or is eating merely an opportunity to fill up the tank as quickly and easily as possible so as to get on with the day? Or perhaps it's an opportunity for numbing, dispelling the gnawing inside? Ceremony or ritual can structure our awareness to be awake and aware, to be alert, knowing that without our conscious focus, we could find ourselves prone to disorder, to being swept away. Having ceremony can mean having a place at the table, and feeling welcome there can be an immense gift.

Lacking any formal or traditional ceremony, we often generate our own unconscious habits, such as eating while driving or in front of the television. And often these habits fall short of providing the well-being that the greater structure of more traditional ceremony provides. Our default behavior gets us through without necessarily nourishing body, mind, and spirit. What's nourishing about ceremony is not just the food, but our kind, caring, respectful awareness attuned to the activities that give life to life. Ceremony can be one way to bring "kind mind" alive.

Thirty years ago the *Wall Street Journal* reported that "even canned corn stumps modern cooks." The article described how one company took the directions off of their canned corn but then got so many complaints that they put the directions back: "Put corn in saucepan on heated burner." One friend queried me further: Do you drain the corn or not? A companion article discussed how much people will pay *not* to cook—that is, to have the same raw ingredients already prepared for you. The conclusion was that people would pay three to five times as much. By now it's probably a great deal more.

Ceremony? Put the food in the oven or microwave and listen for the timer to go off. Again, it's ceremony on the fly that does not provide the opportunity to learn how to stabilize and focus our awareness on relating with the material world; instead, we simply fall prey to expediency.

On a book tour several years back, I met Amy Ahrensdorf in Phoenix, who was devoting herself to teaching mothers to cook—thank you for your efforts, Amy! Many university studies show, she said, that children from families that eat together do better in school, with fewer alcohol and addiction issues. We are nourished when we sit down at the table to eat with our family and friends.

What Amy discovered, somewhat to her surprise and bewilderment, was that to teach cooking she needed to start with even more basic skills: scheduling, budgeting, menu planning, shopping, and some simple meals along with perhaps some more elaborate ones. There are skillful ways to structure reality, which can be seen as very much related to ceremony. It's not just doing what you want when you want to do it, but doing enough of the basics to keep your life from going off the tracks—or as Suzuki Roshi once told me, "If your life is not going forward, it's going downhill . . . backwards."

If you choose to do so, please sort out which activities truly nourish your well-being. You may notice that these are not the same as the activities designed to bring you a more dashing reputation or a respite from responsibilities. One of my teachers (in the world of alchemy), for instance, realized that to know what she was actually eating, she needed to prepare the food herself. Food products, she discovered, conceal too many secrets—it turned out that the canned split-pea soup she was eating at lunch had more sugar than ice cream. She found the meal preparation itself nourishing and discovered she was enjoying not just better meals but also the shopping, the preparation of the food, and the cleaning up. Her life was full of more life—happily so!

———⟶

Learning to Eat with Awareness

Zen practice aims to undo and redo habits of mind and body that do not serve us well, and curiously enough, one aspect of accomplishing this involves the surfacing of our weak points. It's not enough to set up standards and protocols of good behavior and to expect compliance. We need to go through the fire, through the flood, through those places where we are under duress and cannot manage well. Where do we break down—shoulders, back, knees, hips, breathing, digestion—and where do we act out or go unconscious? Confronted with our lapses, we study how to do things more usefully and wisely. I may have come from a family that ate together, which was a good start, but Zen practice is challenging enough that no one can breeze through. I certainly didn't.

One place for meeting our untamed proclivities is mealtime. A Zen meal, as I described earlier, has a great deal of ceremony and only seven or eight minutes to actually eat. Under the circumstances back at Tassajara in the sixties and seventies, we were starved. Mealtimes were the sole occasion for eating. In those years, there were no snack foods—which are now provided at the back door of the kitchen. Few impulse or snacking items were available, unless you ordered them on the town trip, which you could do perhaps twice a month. One student once managed to get an order of roast chicken along with a canned cola!

Meals in the zendo often resembled the lineup at the beginning of a race, where everyone awaited the sound of the starting pistol. The sounding of the clackers—two wooden blocks struck together—announcing eating also signaled a frenzy of activity. Though others were similarly energized, the race was with yourself: to get the food in your mouth as fast as you could and swallow as soon as possible. If you wanted seconds when they were served, you had to be done with your firsts, so practically speaking, you usually had to decide which bowl needed to be emptied quickest, as it was rarely possible to empty all three in time for the second serving. And even if you could, you would not be able to finish all of the seconds before it was time to clean the bowls. What an embarrassment that would be: if everyone else was finished, bowls washed and reassembled, and they were looking at you, the person who was not finished and was keeping them waiting to leave the hall.

Lunch was by far the most competitive meal. Intense emotions flooded the meditation hall, and it all took place in silence. Several kinds of bread, both yeasted and unyeasted, were served in a basket for three people to share. If you were the first of the three, would you take a modest helping and hope the basket would return later in the meal, or would you count the slices, divide by three, and take your share? And if you were the second of the three people, would you take half regardless of how much the first person had taken?

A similar dilemma came with the dishes of spread, frequently based on peanut butter, cream cheese, or perhaps hummus.

Often a student would simply excavate their portion from the serving dish and put it into their bread bowl. It didn't matter whether you could spread it on your bread, because you could always eat it with your spoon.

Amazingly enough, in a single lunch, many of us commonly ate sixteen to eighteen half-slices of bread—sometimes more. That's eight or nine full slices of dense, full-bodied, homemade bread. And we were still famished. My weight dropped to 125 pounds from its accustomed 140. We were like "hungry ghosts," those beings with insatiable appetites but way too narrow throats.

What I came to realize was that I wasn't merely putting food in my mouth—I was shoveling it in. I wasn't tasting the food—I was making it disappear from my mouth as fast as possible. And I wasn't enjoying my food; instead, with a grim determination, I was obsessed with chasing after more—and to get more, you had to make what you had disappear. Given the few minutes we had for eating, nothing else seemed possible if you wanted to get enough food. In this writing I've given rather concise expression to what was going on under the circumstances, but what is probably not clear is just how lost and confused and overwhelmed I was while in the grip of this intense hungering beast—which apparently was me!

Following a lot of struggle and torment, I found myself deciding to eat more slowly—to allow for joy and ease, to practice tasting, and to sense gratitude. When I began tasting and chewing each bite of food, almost immediately I was eating half as much yet feeling satisfied, almost as if the tasting itself was nourishing, along with the kind of food and its quantity. I began to find joy in the experience of eating—awareness resonating, humming with the tasting. Also, the sense of ease became more palpable, as I was settled here in the moment rather than chasing a future moment that was never going to arrive. Eating more closely and intimately brought along a sense of gratitude as well—just this, just this, just this. We give thanks for this food!

—

Please Enjoy Your Food

What I've come to realize over the years is the importance of enjoying food. At Saturday meditation retreats, when we break for lunch, I often tell people, "Please enjoy your food." Much of the morning I have been offering instructions in sitting and walking meditation, and by lunchtime, we may also have had an hour of yoga or qi gong with further directives, so I'd rather keep any further instruction to a minimum. I also don't want eating to be another chore or yet another place to worry about whether or not you are doing it "right." Many of us do enough of that already, so I invite people to "please enjoy your food." I'm referring here to the Buddhist conception of joy, which is described as awareness resonating with or being moved by the object of awareness.

Cultivating the practice of simple enjoyment can be remarkably powerful, yet it is commonly misunderstood. As many of us are accustomed to viewing things objectively rather than subjectively, we have had little opportunity or permission to experience joy and to notice how joy offers a way for our awareness to connect with objects as they appear, whether the objects are things of the world, such as food and other people, or our own internal experience. This resonating or connecting with *other* is often profoundly satisfying, so that we feel truly nourished—which is not at all the same as experiencing things objectively.

The more that connection is lacking, the more we try to control the objective world and with varying degrees of force make it do our bidding. We judge, assess, and evaluate things, grasping for those higher on our value scale and pushing away those that are lower, believing it is our job to amass better experiences. Often this habit produces stress as our collection of experiences does not seem to be good enough and we strive to do better.

On the other hand, when joy is present, our awareness settles down and is less likely to look for something else, something better than *this* to chase after. What a relief—and what a joy!

One caution is that joy itself may quickly shape-shift into greed. As one of my students once commented, "If I enjoyed my food, I'd be a blimp." "No," I attempted to explain, "if you were truly enjoying your food, you'd stop when joy was no longer present. You'd catch yourself shifting into excitement and greed—pause—and come back to joy."

What happens is that joy itself becomes another object to be grasped. Once joy appears, our awareness can mistakenly treat it as an object to be acquired—how exciting—and we may believe that the way to get more of it is to eat faster, swallow more quickly, getting rid of what we have so that we can get more of what we are now mistakenly labeling joy. As we find ourselves in the grip of shoveling in more food while chasing after the joy that is no longer there, the joy is long gone. Excitement and greed, as energizing and gripping as they are, have landed us in a world of deprivation. Joy offers connection and well-being as well as a world of abundance. So being able to distinguish joy from greed and lust becomes pivotally important if you are interested in connection and well-being.

When we enjoy our food, we will tend to be happy and well nourished by what we eat. We may naturally find ourselves meditating. To enjoy something, we need to experience it closely, so we will be giving our attention to what we are eating, noticing flavors and textures and nuances of taste. And we may find ourselves focusing on how to remain present with joy rather than being carried away with greed and excitement, how to be connecting warmheartedly rather than numbing ourselves with food and feeling that we are in the grip of something faceless and demanding. When we are immersed in joy, we no longer miss what we are eating in the present and grasp after future possibilities. We actually have our experience, and having our experience, we have satisfaction. We put the fork down.

As we enter more deeply into enjoyment, we relax and open our hearts to food rather than treating it as an object to be assessed as good or bad, healthy or harmful, or perhaps even as sinful or indulgent. When we are busy making assessments is when we handle and eat food in accordance with what we have attributed to the food. We ignore or overlook the potential for deeper connection with food, the potential for good-heartedness and gratitude that comes with relating through our hearts and our felt sense. When we enjoy our food, we can rest and digest rather than stressing in our pursuit of better experiences.

Powerful! By simply enjoying our food, we let go of many of our judgments of right and wrong and our assessments of "how well am I doing?" or "have I measured up yet?" Enjoying our food may be the best meditation we do all day. Following the path of pleasure is deep and profound and richly rewarding. Potentially, it all takes care of itself without our having to try too hard.

Sometimes people complain that it doesn't work that way, that one needs discipline, austerity, and restraint. Perhaps these are useful in their place, yet too often these rigorous aspects of mind demand overcompliance, insisting that there will be absolutely no lightness. These aspects also imply that our inherent being lacks wisdom or any sense of beauty and consequently needs to be kept in line, restrained, tamed, subdued. For most of us, as we get in touch with our inner aesthetic, we learn to set aside what is not in accord with it. When we stop beating ourselves up, we begin to notice our inherent sweetness of heart.

Many problems that arise in the pursuit of pleasure are due to a lack of devotion, to not being fully enough committed to pleasure, to connection. We put the problem on the object by labeling it sinful or decadent rather than acknowledging how *we* lose ourselves. Which bite of chocolate cake is no longer pleasurable? Which swallow of wine is bringing us down instead of up? Sure, restraint and discipline are needed, but not to deny pleasure, rather to curb excitement and greed when it runs away with us. Use restraint as needed for braking, rather than keeping the brakes on as a way of life!

Please enjoy your food. When pleasure or enjoyment are harshly forbidden, we look for stupor, for unconsciousness, which is the closest we can get to relief from the misplaced drive to discipline and restraint and the overriding admonition not to have any fun. "Watch yourself! If I catch you having fun, I'll make you pay for it." Most often we come by these negative admonitions honestly through our early experiences in life. Still it is not too late to change, to enjoy our food.

In one of my cooking classes, we may make several different tomato sauces, adding one ingredient at a time as a way to observe and learn about flavors. Many people find this study of what makes something taste the way it does quite fascinating, yet when people are preoccupied with all the dos and don'ts of what to eat and what not to eat, then carefully tasting something just means a delay in finally getting to eat. When we are not carefully tasting, the act of eating is no longer something we experience but something that we try to govern better, something we attempt to rule. You try to eat what you're supposed to eat, and if you don't, you're bad. Then it's not surprising that eating or drinking to numbness becomes the best way to quiet the petty tyrant inside who's incessantly passing judgments and dispensing directives. Unfortunately, this going numb from overindulgence only reinforces the petty tyrant's claim that you need more discipline—when what you really could use is permission to have some simple enjoyment.

And so, dear tyrant, please, if you would, allow for enjoyment; and being softly alert, please keep an eye out for when enjoyment has morphed into greed.

The ironic thing, of course, is that for the most part, we are such sweet, good-hearted people, and we deserve everyday joys and pleasures of simple, wholesome foods coming to us with our caring attention. Here you are, my precious! Please enjoy.

~~~

Ingredients for Living Fully

Recently I came across a quote from William Blake:

> . . . the whole creation will . . . appear infinite and holy, whereas it now appears finite and corrupt. This will come to pass by an improvement of sensual enjoyment.

We've been going in the opposite direction!

Eating, restored to a rightful prominence, central to life and living, could be a sacrament, an occasion for celebrating and promoting life. Enlightened eating is to live from the heart rather than the head, to engage passion and gusto in the process, to refine greed into pleasure, to taste with relish and gratitude. Eating well and in good company is basic to nourishment, source, and sustenance. Here are all the ingredients for fully living: celebration, sanctity, ritual, passion, fulfillment, contentment. Along with these come enjoyment and clear-minded discrimination, interest, curiosity, and discovery. To eat well is to reown your humanness, what Rumi calls the "exquisite vitality" of a human being. This is to enter the present moment and fulfill the present moment. It's yours for the asking and for the giving.

To eat well is to take in experience and digest it—not just food but also feelings, thoughts, judgments, sights, sounds, people, and things—to take in and digest the present moment of experience. Digesting is extracting the nutritive essence from what you have taken in and discarding what you cannot use, discarding what cannot become you.

What We Taste "In-forms" Us

Nothing in the universe is hidden. When you taste what goes into your mouth, everything is there: life and death, joy and sorrow, earth and sky, sunlight and darkness, hope and fear, satisfaction and disappointment. You can taste all of this to the extent you are willing, or you can go unconscious to some extent and hope for the best. Unfortunately, going unconscious often means that we are not present enough to make wholesome, nourishing food choices. When the foods we choose are not inherently satisfying and fulfilling, we may overeat.

To practice tasting what we put in our mouths and to make that experience the basis for our food choices means we could discover the wisdom of the body, the wisdom of experiencing things closely.

We can taste salty, sweet, sour, bitter, and pungent: the salt of olives, hard cheeses, soy sauce, and to a lesser degree the salt of onions, carrots, celery, and parsley (which in a concentrated dried form are used in salt substitutes); the sweet of grains, potatoes, yams, winter squashes, and dried fruits; the sour or tart of lemon, strawberry, raspberry, apples, oranges, and balsamic vinegar; the bitter of walnuts, grapefruit, chocolate, and winter greens; the pungent of black and red peppers, green chilies, garlic, and ginger. We can taste earth, stem, leaf, flower, and fruit.

What we taste in-forms us. What we taste is personal and not objective or scientific. It's ours.

14

DO NOT SEE WITH ORDINARY EYES, DO NOT THINK WITH ORDINARY MIND

One obstacle in cooking is that you may want the results guaranteed to reflect well on you, but you cannot be sure that they will. Food is so intimately associated with self that without the guarantee of approval, the risk of rejection appears unacceptable. Work—putting yourself on the line—means risking failure. You worry, especially ahead of time. It might turn out that you will be seen as incompetent, incapable, uncreative, or just a plain stupid, dumb idiot who should have known better or done better, like all the others who are so much more skillful than you. Your default position becomes fulfilling assignments (perhaps from a cookbook) and aiming for a good grade. Either that or concluding, "I don't have time to cook."

Do Not See with Ordinary Eyes,
Do Not Think with Ordinary Mind

*If this is not yet clear to you, it is because your thoughts
run around like a wild horse and your feelings jump
about like a monkey in the forest. When the monkey
and horse step back and reflect upon themselves,
freedom from all discrimination is realized naturally.*

ZEN MASTER DŌGEN

As with meditation, cooking is not a matter of getting or
having, but a vehicle, a mode of manifesting your innate good
heart and benevolent hands. Your spirit becomes food, food
for yourself and food for others: very immediately, very directly
you give life to life. How sweet is that? You offer what you have
to offer.

Yet complaints may surface that your cooking is not delicious enough or not what the others want. You may find the
results unsatisfying. The work of cooking seems to have taken
way too long, plus you are tired and out of sorts. Why doesn't
someone cook for you? You're worth it. Cooking is so much
work, and where is the satisfaction and fulfillment in that?

Zen Master Dōgen advised, "Do not see with ordinary eyes.
Do not think with ordinary mind."

What finally is worth doing? Worth the trouble that comes
with it? Where will you put your attention? your effort? your
heart? your hands? How will you decide?

With all the marketing in our culture, exorbitant effort
and money are put into grabbing your attention. Such irony:

grabbing your attention with product, entertainment, and pitch, and then charging you money to have your attention grabbed. Where, we wonder, is the next attention-grabber that will really "do it" for us?

Ordinary thought does not notice the possibility of choosing where to put your attention rather than having it swept away, or at least mildly amused—your time filled with ongoing divertissements. Beyond the scope of ordinary eyes, not thinking with ordinary mind, you may see that the gift of your attention makes things precious—that is, the gift of your attention attuned to receiving what is *other* begins to develop wholesome relationships, with others, with food, with the world.

With your attention attuned to receiving, you can taste the true spirit of the grain, the sweet, earthy sunniness of carrot. Beyond the measuring, evaluating, assessing that the ordinary mind excels at, you're connecting with what is beyond ordinary thinking, an indescribable turning, the cosmic hum, vibrant, spacious, vast. With your awareness attuned to receiving, to offering, you'll bring heaven down to earth—and you'll have something to eat.

Food Is Precious

Do not think with ordinary mind; turn a sixteen-foot
golden buddha into a leaf of cabbage; value food as
though it was your eyesight.

ZEN MASTER DŌGEN

To say that "food is precious" is not quite right. What is precious, if anything, is our capacity to experience food as precious! Not knowing what is precious, we may struggle for more money or greater recognition or perhaps simply for getting through the day. All well and good—important work here on planet Earth. "It's going great." "It's going poorly." Some triumphs perhaps, a few fiascoes. We're getting by—though we may rarely be finding anything *precious*. So a deeper aspect of our life journey is to find out what awakens the sense of precious, what brings true meaning or value to the fore. By the way, my use of the word *precious* may be a bit strong; for instance, those at the Shambhala Center in Vienna use the expression *basic goodness*.

Is anyone finding you precious? And what would that look like? Does anyone care about you? Do you? Are you precious and sacred on the spot, without changing anything about your body or mind? Or is there always something not quite right that needs fixing, so that you could not possibly have a warm and kind feeling for your inherent goodness?

Food can be a commodity, a business, or fuel for the human body-machine. Or is it love itself, coming from air and water, earth and sunlight? How do you see it?

In the absence of the sacred, food becomes impersonal. When we do not recognize what is precious, we have strawberries that ship across the country and still have a shelf life of a week, according to the grower, cigar waving in hand, who capped his remarks saying, "But they taste like soap." We have fast food that tastes the same from sea to shining sea. You can take one bite to check and then dependably stop tasting while you finish consuming, noticing perhaps the flavor hooks of salt, sugar, or grease, but not experiencing what's beneath the surface.

What's precious is what you receive as being precious. And ironically, even the soapy strawberries and the same-tasting fast food could possibly be treated as precious. It's just much more of a challenge than with the berries from your backyard or the patch by the pond down the dirt road. What a great adventure and how amazing were those berries when I was six and seven! They stained my hands and face and provided startling, exhilarating, satisfying taste.

It must have been about thirty years ago, when I was a serious student of Iyengar Yoga, that I met one of Mr. Iyengar's foremost teachers, Kofi Busia. At some point, we were discussing food, and Kofi mentioned that while growing up in Ghana they never ate *anonymous* food—they would always know where the ingredients came from, whose farm, whose valley, which hillside. How simple it was to feel at home in that world, to feel that the food was precious. It had taken Kofi years, he said, to get used to eating food that was anonymous. Blessings to you, Kofi; prayers and blessings.

To make food precious, to sanctify it, you need to see it that way—that is, handle it that way and taste it that way. What is precious is you yourself, consciousness itself, your capacity to treat something as precious. To understand that food is precious or sacred is to realize that we are living simultaneously in two worlds, the horizontal world of everyday comparisons and assessments and the vertical world that connects with the Beyond, or the Boundless. Sometimes the world Beyond is called heaven, sometimes the "upper vertical." In the world of alchemy, it is simply called "above": As above, so below. In Zen, sometimes we refer to the Relative and the Absolute, Samsara and Nirvana, Emptiness, or Big Mind.

Relatively speaking, we have large and small, radishes and potatoes, lettuce and spinach, and they have various values depending on the scale we are using: financial, nutritional, color, shape, texture, personal preference. In the world of the Absolute, everything is equally valuable, equally precious. Radishes are not competing with potatoes, and lettuce is not jealous of the spinach. Each is sincerely itself—precious and beyond compare. In the world of the Absolute, we could say that each ingredient is a gift from Beyond. We do not create it, fabricate or manufacture it. (Though now, with gene-modification technology, we believe, rightly or wrongly, that we can improve on the gift, as though it were ours. Sometimes that's called hubris.)

For gifts from Beyond, we give thanks, praise, and gratitude unconditionally. When in the world of the relative, we assess, measure, and compare. Sometimes we believe that if we are select enough and skillful enough, we can offer the very best food. Still, it is speaking relatively: pick everything organic, choose baby lettuces and baby carrots, eat only the finest, prepare with care and attention. At times, it seems that even precious itself has become a commodity, and we are living in the realm of the gods where our slightest whim can be satisfied—as long as we can afford it. Fine restaurants are primed to provide religious experiences, and huge organic grocery stores feel like modern cathedrals. Dining and shopping become holy pilgrimages.

Yet at this time of experiencing the food judged best, are we giving thanks? Thanks to the wondrous, inexplicable mystery of Life giving life to life? Or are we still battling to gain what is better, what is best, glorying in our standing—while not understanding that what is precious about food is seeing and tasting its inherent goodness. This comes when no longer chasing after the next big thing, but pausing instead to quietly taste what is in your mouth, allowing what is even larger-hearted to unfold—celebrating a being-at-one-with the Sacred. Chefs often do this, as they are moved and touched by the ingredients, as they taste what comes from earth and sea, as they go out to the fields and meet the growers.

We confuse the two worlds! Our ability to experience something as sacred is not the same as our capacity to evaluate the ingredients or the results. If only the best is worthy of praise and gratitude, then no wonder many of us are plagued with low self-esteem and way too often a level of self-hatred that seems to necessitate numbing with alcohol and television. We do not measure up to the standards we apply, while at the same time, we are not experiencing our fundamental good-heartedness, which is beyond compare. You may sometimes feel that you're only as good as your last meal, your last performance, but at the same time, you can study how to care for what is small and less than magnificent.

Agreeing to Love Yourself

Your loving doesn't know its majesty until it knows its helplessness.
RUMI

Whether in the kitchen or in our daily lives, emotional habits can remain nearly impossible to alter. Habitual thinking often remains firmly in place. Certainly on the spot, in the flood of feelings, the capacity to reflect may be severely limited. To shift, we may need help, help from outside or perhaps in the form of hitting the wall, when we have no alternative but to take a break, and then reflection may ensue.

This happened to me in the sixties when I was the cook at Tassajara. I found myself in bed unable to move. I'd labored mightily to provide meals, aiming to surpass myself. Each time a meal is "good," you've raised the bar, and those praising you ask, "How will you surpass that?" I kept going until finally I couldn't, staying in my bed, with its rumpled army blankets and sheets no longer crisp and white. In my early twenties keeping my cabin clean and welcoming was not much of a priority. The floor that we'd painted a bright, grassy, porch green was dusty and dull. The bare wood walls silently stared back at me. Originally built to be a vacation cottage, it had no insulation against heat in the summer or cold in the winter, and the screened openings in the wall were now covered with heavy-duty weathered plastic that was staple-gunned to wooden frames.

How will I ever be able to cook and please everybody? Slowly, thoughts unraveled, each responding to the previous one. *It is impossible to please everyone, absolutely impossible. But I want to please everyone! Really. Why would you want to do that?* My thinking had become self-reflective, questioning itself. I needed to come up with something to explain my wish to please. *If I please them, then they will love me.* An immediate response: *You really think so? They don't love you. They love the food, and they don't know you or what you go through to prepare meals.*

The air in my room was heavy, a large beast pressing me down. In the summer months, I could take down the plastic window substitutes at night to let cool mountain air into the room. In the morning, before the heat of the day, I would replace them on their nails, which were bent in the middle and could be twisted one way or the other to secure the framed plastic or to let it loose. With the plastic up, the room was cool until one or two in the afternoon, when it would become hot and stuffy.

My inner dialogue continued: *They don't care about you in the slightest. They could not care less. When the meal bell rings, you serve them their food. That's all they care about, satisfying their hunger. They don't care whether or not you feel like cooking, they are not concerned whether you're sad or anxious, stressed or unhappy. Their message clearly says, bring us our breakfast, our lunch, our dinner—make it good and on time! The world, my friend, is an insatiable beast, even your friends and loved ones. "Perform," they say, "that's your job. And a good cook will do his job without asking for help."*

You find out a great deal about your thinking when you've been flattened.

The blurred plastic on the windows prevented seeing out. Nobody came by to visit. My body was worn and ragged. I had agreed to the demands.

Keep it together, I had told myself. *Keep going until you can't go anymore.* And now I could not continue. Why would I ever get up again? *No matter how hard I work, I will not be able to gain their love. Yet as long as I slave for them, they'll let me stay.*

The inner inquiry continued: *And why would I want their love?* The answer came almost immediately: *If they loved me enough, I could accumulate enough evidence to love myself!* This surprised me, that I don't love myself. But perhaps with enough evidence I could be convinced.

The dirty room, the unwashed linen, the oppressive heat, and the inner dialogue continued: *Oh worthless piece of a piece of discarded garbage, how could you be lovable? What have you ever done?* Here I was defaming myself, but after all, don't we need to perform and be accomplished to be loved?

It turns out that's what I was doing: skillful self-disparagement. *And whose job is it,* I wondered, *to do something differently?* I guess that it's up to me to love myself without any evidence. No one else seems to want the job—or even to be the least bit interested in the task. If I want to love myself, I'll need to learn how to love myself without any conditions. It's up to me. There's no other way. It's that simple.

And it's not about cooking! Even the evidence that people like the food is not evidence that they love me. If I want to love myself, I'll need to start loving myself. Given that I appear to completely lack the capacity for loving myself—starting from zero—this seems like such an improbably impossible task.

Still and all, what will it take? To give my heart to my heart?

It's such a huge task, where will I start? Perhaps I could begin with tenderly kneading the bread dough, with cutting one hundred thousand onions, carrots, and celery stalks. I could start with seeing the sincerity of teapots, I could see the blessedness of food and offer it to others. I could take care of leftovers.

Tired and overwhelmed with feelings, did anything matter? Yes—it turned out that learning to love myself, one precious moment at a time mattered. Learning to appreciate my good-hearted effort.

15

AROUSING JOY
AND WELL-BEING

Use your way-seeking
mind carefully to vary
the menus from time to time
and offer the great assembly
ease and comfort.

ZEN MASTER DŌGEN

Men at Work Cooking:
A Bachelor Party Dinner

One of my most satisfying cooking classes was for a bachelor party. Rather last minute, my friend Charlie Sheppard called to invite me to teach. The party was scheduled for a Monday evening, and I already had a class scheduled for Tuesday, so I expressed reluctance to Charlie. The man is brilliant, and more importantly in this case, he has excellent boundaries. He wasn't going to try to talk me into anything or sell me on what a good idea it would be. "It's up to you, Ed," he explained over the phone. "Name your price."

"That helps," I told him. "Although money is not the most important thing, it definitely plays a part. I teach if I feel drawn to doing it."

After I expressed again my reservations about the short notice as well as having another event scheduled for the next evening, Charlie didn't tell me, as some people might have, that those were not good enough excuses to turn him down. Instead, he agreed that it might be challenging but also suggested that it would be a fine adventure: men cooking together. I was still hesitant, weighing what to do. Finally, Charlie repeated that it was up to me and gave me a choice: "Ed, it's either you or Marin Joe's. Nothing against Marin Joe's, but we'd rather have you." That settled it, as a wave of willingness washed through me.

Classes are always stressful and demand great attention to detail, as well as alertness, responsiveness, and focus. I may be in charge, but I am often bringing boxes of groceries to an unfamiliar address and an untested kitchen. I am in the dark about where the bowls reside, the mixing spoons, the vegetable peelers (if there are any), the pots and pans. From experience, I know to bring my sharp knives for everyone to use and heat-resistant rubber spatulas for cleaning pans and bowls so that we leave almost no trace to be washed down the drain. I pop a few cutting boards into my well-used banana boxes, along with fresh sponges (yes, many well-equipped kitchens have nothing to clean with). For Charlie's, I also packed some round pizza pans and fluted, removable-bottom tart pans.

I prefer teaching hands-on cooking rather than demo cooking or cooking for entertainment. I want people to participate, to lend a hand. Actually doing it seems more crucial to learning to cook than reading recipes or watching cooking shows. Also, I've found that the more wine served during class, the less participation, the more chattering. I enjoy wine too, but mostly I need to wait for dinner to start to begin tasting, or I will not be able to hold the room, follow through with the menu plans, and keep the class on track.

Students with the mind that seeks the way are often difficult to find; however, my guys wanted to cook, to study, to learn. Most of the guys at the party hardly ever cooked, but they loved handling the sharp knives and learning how to use them with some dexterity. While we worked together, a tender sweetness began to flavor the room. I divided up the menu so that each man largely worked on a particular dish. Men may be stereotyped as being tough and cold, but they have your back, and when they feel safe and at ease, their hearts may flower. Unfortunately, there are way too few occasions where men feel safe, where they will not be subjected to being shamed and to people finding fault with their efforts. But that evening we "rested in the immediate as though it were infinity," as Donald Babcock says in his poem "The Little Duck."

I confess: we did prepare some playful bachelor-party dishes by working carefully on how we assembled the ingredients. Platters of fresh asparagus, lightly blanched, were arranged with the stalks pointing in the same direction down the middle of the platter and widening out at the base. Lemon-scented mayonnaise was arrayed around the other end of the platter, accenting the tip ends of the asparagus.

A caprese salad had a similar theme, with tomato rounds overlapping in a straight line down the middle of the platter, two circles of tomato slices at one end, and the fresh mozzarella slices arcing around the other end. Julienne strips of basil primarily decorated the tomato end of the platter. A light vinaigrette garnished everything right before serving so that the salt in the dressing did not have time to draw a lot of water out of the tomatoes. Our group found we could focus on this task with ease, delighting in our capacity to be artists breaking out of the mold.

A third dish emphasized an oval format, using cantaloupe slices, avocado slices, and roasted red pepper. It's a dish with a simple concept that blossoms with flavors and color: the sweet, refreshing, pale orange fruit of the cantaloupe; the smooth, oily, earth green of the avocado; the vibrant, viney, slightly smokey, bright red of the peppers—yum! We cut open the cantaloupe, scooped out the seeds, and again, men at work carefully cut off the peels following the round of the melon. I showed them how to cut the melon halves diagonally instead of straight down: beautiful round fillets of fruit increasing in size with some sliced orange U's to finish. These were marinated in sugar and lime juice with a touch of salt.

The red peppers we roasted and peeled before slicing in strips and seasoning with a hint of garlic, along with olive oil, balsamic vinegar, salt, and pepper. I season to my taste, so for me, just a hint of garlic or you start losing the sweet pepper flavor.

The avocados were cut in half, twisted open, and then—another use for my heat-resistant rubber spatulas—we delicately separated the flesh from the peel. We cut the avocado halves diagonally, and they were ready for assembly.

First the cantaloupe rounds overlapping each other create arcs down opposite sides of a large serving platter, meeting at each end. Then the avocado slices were fanned out along the inner edges of the cantaloupe, while the roasted red-pepper slices were shaped in an inner oval. A light shallot vinaigrette went over the top, especially on the avocado slices. Sometimes I garnish lightly with thin julienne strips of cilantro or spearmint.

Not everyone sees this oval shape as particularly evocative, but the gentlemen in my class were happily enthralled. Sometimes I've served this salad, and no one says a thing, either out of obliviousness or politeness. After all, we are eating! And perhaps it is better to overlook some of the sensual aspects of food rather than voice them.

Assembling pizzas is always enjoyable, as everyone is suddenly transformed into an artist: perhaps sautéed mushrooms, grilled slices of zucchini, and eggplant seasoned with salt and balsamic vinegar, or lemon juice, plus something pungent, maybe fresh ginger for zucchini and black pepper for the eggplant. Once the dough was rolled out (having been kneaded a couple of hours earlier), we coated it with olive oil heavily infused with garlic. Then perhaps two or three cheeses of choice were placed in their own area to maintain their distinctive flavor (or not if nondairy was requested), followed by the arrangement of the vegetables. Every bite different! After baking, we added freshly grated Asiago cheese (which in my generics-priced life has more flavor than similarly priced Parmesan), along with some minced fresh herbs, usually oregano, thyme, or both, and occasionally basil.

The fresh fruit tarts were made early during the meal prep, well before the last-minute stress of getting the meal together. Flour with butter, sugar, lemon peel, and vanilla extract—the dough was pressed into the tart pans. Everybody needs to learn to press the dough into the sides at the *bottom* of the pan so that it pushes up the sides and can be pinched off at the top. If you're ever in one of my classes, I can show you, though many need further instruction or practice.

After the tart was baked unadorned, we let it cool slightly and then smoothed out the spread. Egg custard is most traditional, but I love fresh cream cheese seasoned with lemon juice and honey. In Germany and Austria, I have used Quark or Topfen, which is even better because along with its mild fragrance and flavor, it is much more mixable and spreadable than the gummy American cream cheese. Fresh strawberries were our fruit of choice, seasoned—and tasted as we went along—with maple syrup, a few drops of balsamic vinegar, and a gentle grating of black pepper. The goal is to make the strawberries taste even more like strawberries, so it's important to taste the strawberries at the start to see what you can notice while you taste. You don't want to taste vinegar or pepper, but the essence of strawberry.

Several of the men mentioned that Eric should help with the dessert, and while we worked, Eric explained that when he was a small boy, seven years old, he loved to bake. One day he made cupcakes for another boy's birthday party at school. "They were so good, tender and flavorful, fresh from home. Everybody loved them! And then the teacher said, 'Eric, those cupcakes are really delicious. If you keep this up, one day you'll make someone a wonderful wife.'" Eric never went into the kitchen again.

Often at about that age we are shamed over our efforts—"What's that supposed to be?" someone will demand in response to our sincere efforts in art. Quite possibly, Eric's teacher was trying to make a joke, but Eric heard shame and stayed out of the kitchen. Later, when he got married, Eric said, "I did what my father did: I made waffles on Sunday and did some outdoor grilling." Finally, at the age of thirty-seven, he remembered what had happened and realized he could bake again. Thirty years had passed, and finally, baking was safe from shaming. What an auspicious realization, that he could give his heart to something and not be told that he was damaged, defective, or insufficiently masculine.

A fine, long table setting greeted the twelve of us for dinner. After we sat down, Charlie told us that following dinner and before dessert we would each be invited to share what had been most pivotal and important in our long-term relationships with women. An astonishing evening awaited us. We offered toasts to the upcoming marriage, I shared my Buddhist-flavored meal prayer, and we commenced eating. When I glanced across the table near the start of the meal, the man there was sitting in stunned silence, tears welling up in his eyes. He'd eaten a bite of the pizza, and the remainder of the slice remained immobile a few inches from his mouth. When we turned to give him our attention, he stammered, "I think that *this* is the best pizza I've ever eaten." Yes, it was good, but what had made it the best ever was that *he* had made it. With his eyes and ears, nose and tongue, with his good-hearted effort, this man had made something ever so delicious. Oh, what an awakening!

Along with the pizza, we passed around the platters of asparagus and caprese salad and the plates of composed cantaloupe and avocado salad. With our conscientious devotion, we had prepared a fully flavored meal to nourish ourselves. The sweetness of our laboring together permeated the food, the wine, the water. We were graced. Yes, we were enjoying the food, but we were also awestruck that we could prepare such deliciousness ourselves.

With the meal winding down, Charlie spoke up to let us know that the time had come for each of us to share what had been most important in our long-term relationships with women. The father of the groom was one of the first, saying that he had been married twice: once for fifteen years and presently for sixteen years. The relationships had been a gift. He had been honored to devote himself to his partners and to their mutual fulfillment—not always successfully, but he'd done his best in the ways he knew how.

One after another, each man attested to the primary and pivotal importance of his committed relationships with women. At least one man had experienced problems with addiction, but with the support of his partner, he had seen his way through it. Another expressed that he had felt rather scattered in his life without the focus of a committed relationship.

The testimonials were a touching tribute to the men's dedication to their long-term relationships, to their commitment and positive intentions. Again and again, the men around the dining table would aver that sharing love with a woman was central in their lives. Things had not always gone well, but they had been willing to learn, make sacrifices, and recommit. Last to speak was the father of the bride, who announced that he had been married for thirty-one years, and then he paused before giving the punch line, "to the same woman." We all laughed, as the first father had also been married for thirty-one years, but to two different women. The father of the bride and his wife had fallen in love as teenagers in Cuba and decided then that they wanted to spend their lives together. Escaping to the United States led to years of ongoing challenges: learning the English language, finding work, locating places to live, as well as times of emotional discord. His story riveted the room, and when he ended by saying, "Of all the things I've accomplished in my life, I'm proudest of my marriage," most of us burst into tears.

Strawberry tart followed, with more good wishes to the bridegroom. While we were cleaning up, a man approached me to say, "Last year my wife and I spent six weeks traveling around France, eating fresh fruit tarts, but tonight's tart was better than anything we had that whole trip. Thank you. This has been an incredible evening."

You're welcome.

16

HANDLING LEFTOVERS

Purifying Our Love

We practice Zen to purify our love.
SUZUKI ROSHI

In *The Unsettling of America*, Wendell Berry's premise is that a significant portion of American culture over its lifetime has been characterized by the mind of exploitation. We get what we can get out of a situation, place, relationship, and then we move on, heading west into the setting sun. We don't have to clean up the mess we left behind, whether it's pollution, land laid to waste, or relationships gone sour. We're on the make, setting out to hit our next score, or to score on our next hit. Always there are greener pastures, unadulterated with our previous presence—pastures that we are seeking to exploit for our own profit, without concern for the costs in human misery or despoliation of the earth. Without acknowledging side effects or collateral damage, we use it up, wear it out, make do, do without, and move on. We also call this capitalism, the free market. People make money at the expense of others, at the cost of the environment.

Berry contrasts this with the mind of nurturing, when we're in it for the long haul, tending the garden as it grows, watching over our children as they mature into adulthood. We clean up after ourselves, so that we have a decent place to live—there's no moving on to what has not yet been spoiled. We cultivate caring and compassion for others, so that we live in a harmonious community. We attend to our spiritual life, so that we have direction that comes from within and beyond—and not just the incentive to profit at the expense of others.

"We practice Zen," Suzuki Roshi explained one morning in the old Tassajara zendo, "to purify our love." He elaborated, "Usually our love is associated with some idea of gain—what will we get out of it?" As we purify our love, we are shifting from the mind of exploitation to the mind of nurturing. We shift from our head to our heart, from thinking (about how to get and have) to feeling (how to connect and benefit ourselves and others).

This is not about what you should or shouldn't do—"Be kind" or "Don't be selfish"—but rather about choosing where to put your awareness and noticing that where you put your awareness can be like a gift or a blessing. When you can share the goodness that is inside with the world outside, then the garden grows, the food arrives, and your family flourishes.

The kitchen can be a place for purifying your love, shifting your thinking from what you can get out of it, to how you can offer your time while you are there. This is something we keep deciding: how to spend our time. And even the concept of spending your time is already off the mark, as spending probably means you would want to be making great purchases with your accumulated effort. Perhaps "gifting" works better—where will you choose to gift your time?

Using Leftovers

When I was first invited to cook at Tassajara in 1966, Jimmie and Ray taught me how to prepare breakfast and lunch for the guests and the staff. It was the last summer that Tassajara was owned by Bob and Anna Beck, so we were serving eggs and bacon, biscuits, pancakes, and French toast, along with fruit for breakfast, and we turned leftovers into lunch. If you were there for several days, perhaps a week or more, you began to realize that Tuesday's dinner was morphing into Thursday's lunch, and Wednesday's supper was rematerializing as Friday's midday meal.

A roast turkey became soup, with a stock prepared by simmering the bones with onion, celery, carrot, salt, and seasonings. Leftover meat and vegetables were cut into spoon-sized pieces and added, along with freshly sautéed onions and garlic, perhaps along with diced carrot and celery. Wine might be used to deglaze the sautéed-onion pan. Salt and seasonings were adjusted, soy sauce might be added for color and flavor, or perhaps some tomato paste would grace the soup with a richer color and taste. Rice might become fried rice or a casserole topped with breadcrumbs or roasted nuts. (Okay—Campbell's Cream of Mushroom Soup might be used for moisture and flavor.) Sometimes vegetable dishes could be turned into a salad with a vinaigrette or a mayonnaise dressing, along with chopped olives or diced celery, green onions or shallots.

We cooked! People have been doing it for centuries. Who could afford to waste food? Serving a dish once and discarding what is uneaten comes with modern affluence. The leftover bread and heels of bread became bread puddings and brown betties, croutons for soup or salad, crumbs for thickening soups, or even bread soup (which is so out of fashion now, but you can Google great traditional recipes). I know that everything cannot be used, that things get overlooked, that food spoils, yet making a sincere effort to care for food is not a matter of perfection but of simple everyday effort and attention.

I still remember the Greek lemon soup in which chicken stock was simmered with leftover rice. Egg beaten with lemon juice added at the end provided sunlight, warmth, and hearty flavor. We beat some hot soup into the egg-and-lemon mixture to heat it gradually so that the eggs did not scramble, before folding it back into the hot soup. Heavenly.

For dessert we often made date-nut bars or brownies, saving time by putting the batter into the pans and later cutting what we baked into squares or bars, rather than taking the time to shape individual cookies.

It seemed obvious: saving and eating leftovers. The first minestrone soup recipe I saw called for a half cup of potatoes and similarly small amounts of pasta, vegetables, and tomato sauce. Good grief! The recipe seemed to imply that you made this soup from scratch, but it made no sense. You sautéed onion with garlic, salt, thyme, and oregano, added a stock (made from your leftover bones), and cleaned out your refrigerator (especially if you'd been cooking Italian). The soup is served with freshly minced parsley and a side of grated Parmesan.

For passato di verdure, you could blend together assorted vegetables, including lettuce—think leftover salad—perhaps fortify the flavors with roasted onions, and serve with croutons, Parmesan, parsley, and a drizzle of olive oil (or whichever of these you had available).

It wasn't much, but when Zen Center invited me to be the head cook at Tassajara, I had a background in working with leftovers. Early on we were told that traditionally in Zen we were to eat our leftovers the same day—just in case we did not survive the night—so for dinner we ate a lot of gruel, which was simply all the leftovers heated together. It wasn't cuisine and was often sour (poor refrigeration contributed), but whatever was left over from that turned out to be an excellent starter for making bread. Using the leftover gruel as liquid, our "gruel bread" turned out to be a kind of sourdough, not needing any yeast for the dough to rise. Leftover morning cereal was also an effective starter for "cereal bread." Though some of these efforts were rather successful, overall I admit the food was probably not that good. Lack of modern refrigeration impeded the process, as did lack of staff, experience, and money. Yet our efforts were sincere and heartfelt.

Since Zen Master Dōgen exhorted the head cook to prepare a soup of wild grasses surpassing those made with cream (or expensive ingredients), lack wasn't much of an excuse. We could easily have seasoned our gruel with garlic, ginger, red chili, soy sauce, and dark sesame oil, or some combination of these, which are not particularly expensive and provide the flavor-rich palette of much East Asian cuisine. Nowadays, I know to rely on these seasonings, and I also know to smell everything that goes into my leftover soups so that anything unpalatable gets composted. The beautiful flavors are enhanced; the slightly off flavors contribute character.

Nowadays, spiritual centers seem to focus on preparing fresh food—leftovers are perhaps reheated one night a week, and then whatever is uneaten is discarded. Apparently we can afford it—that, or we're simply not interested in studying how to use leftovers. Also, most cookbooks explain how to make great dishes using newly procured produce and neglect to speak about using what is left over. Certainly the plethora of food allergies and sensitivities add to the challenge of combining old dishes to make new ones—and if the cooks need to list all the ingredients when serving the food anew, using leftovers may be almost impossible. We've become a people unaccustomed to "eating what is served," the classic Zen encouragement.

People relate variously with leftover food. One excellent chef I know throws away any leftovers because by the time they will be eaten, she says, "They will have lost their vital essence." I also heard from a friend who had been the cook for Swami Muktananda that the guru insisted his food be freshly prepared, which meant his eating within twenty minutes of its readiness, or it was to be prepared again. A meal could be prepared two or three times when the guru's arrival was delayed.

The freshness of the food being served is but one factor. I for one am still practicing as a Zen student: "Receive what is offered. Do not waste a single grain. Treat the food as though it were your eyesight"—this from Zen Master Dōgen. Personally, I find eating food product far more debilitating than eating leftovers.

Some well-known chefs are exemplary in their use of leftovers—or so the story goes. Bill Buford in his marvelous book *Heat* describes how the other chefs in the kitchen dread the appearance of cooking star and head chef Mario Batali. Apparently, he would often head straight for the compost barrel and begin pulling out celery ends, red pepper tops, and other unused items. He would then hold them aloft and browbeat the other chefs: "We're in the restaurant business. We buy food at one price and sell it at another. *This* is our profit. Find a use for it."

My friend Patrick, who is executive chef for a large hotel in Südtirol, tells a similar story about his training when his head chef discovered a slice of hard-boiled egg in the trash—"Find a use for it!" he exhorted. We assume they are nonetheless following the applicable health codes and not reserving food that was left over on individual plates!

The standard expression in Zen is that "if even a layman can work like this, how much more so should we Zen students." Yet in my limited experience, Zen students do not seem to be particularly inspired to undertake this practice, even though one of Zen Master Dōgen's points of emphasis in his *Instructions* encourages us to treat food as though it were our eyesight—literally as though it were our "eyeball." I take this seriously and aim to practice actually doing this while "seeing with my own eyes" and "working with my own hands." It is a practice, Dōgen says, where you "do not fail to place even one speck of dust on the summit of the mountain of wholesome deeds or to add even one drop of water to the ocean of merit."

Your effort to care for the food is what makes it precious.

While cooking at Tassajara, I began reaching for the heat-resistant rubber spatula to clean out pots and scrape off serving platters. I made the assumption that it was spiritual work, yet, spiritual or not, initially I did not want to do it. All manner of verbal resistance arose: *This is stupid. I hate this. What kind of idiot am I?* Essentially, I did not want to waste my time in order not to waste food. Dōgen's words were "not to see with ordinary eyes, not to think with ordinary mind." It seemed that I would need to do this practice in order to open my eyes and awaken my mind, as worldly thinking often does not value leftovers.

The inner resistance was formidable: *Why doesn't someone else care for the leftovers? Doesn't anyone care? Why do I have to be the one to do this?* Nowadays I suspect that caring for leftovers means once again meeting your discards from childhood, those painful experiences that you'd prefer to keep buried. In the face of these objections, I made a choice: *I will care for food; I will take care of it whether or not others choose to do so. I will show others how to do this, that it is possible. What is possible is to act from a place of generosity and compassion.* And if I didn't start small, when would I begin? And, of course, I too often felt small and uncared for. Caring for leftovers meant that I too was worth cherishing.

Somewhere in all my protesting I began thinking more widely. *When I feel like a little piece of a piece of leftover, should I simply discard myself? If I am not at my best, should I look for a compost bucket to toss myself in? Can I always be at my best, or will I work with and offer what I have to offer?* Upon reflection, it appeared that my choosing to exert myself meant that I cared, and if I cared, then I was cared for. If the leftovers were worth saving, I too was worth regarding as precious.

If the small amounts of food are not precious and worthy, are you worthy? Does anyone care? Do you? Do you care about yourself? Doing the work of caring for leftovers was also shifting my worldview. I was freshly reincarnating into a world that cares because I was practicing compassionate attention to small things.

When you are feeling small, and possibly foul-smelling, you could take yourself in hand and offer some tender loving care, enter into your body, find a solid place to put your feet, reinhabit your heart, enjoy your breath, perhaps make yourself a cup of tea.

Not Wasting

*The most important point is to express your true nature
in the simplest, most adequate way and to appreciate
it in the smallest existence.*

SUZUKI ROSHI

Although I am going against the current, I want to share with
you some of the ways that I practice not wasting. For starters,
I buy sensibly, just what we can eat at home. At the homes of
others, I am often struck by opulent displays of fruit, and I
cannot help wondering whether it is also being eaten and not
just used for viewing. They must eat a lot more fruit than I do!

Fifty years later, as I continue to reach for the heat-resistant
rubber spatula, one of my students refers to my doing this as
"Ed-Browning it." Though I rather hope that this does not go
into general parlance, I am grateful when someone notices
and willingly undertakes this practice. Perhaps my practice
of thoroughly cleaning the food out of pots and off of platters is religious fanaticism or rigid compulsion, yet with this
practice, my aesthetic has changed: the time "wasted" while
saving food has become time saved when preparing dishes in
the following days. Rinsing out pots and pans after cooking
with small amounts of water and setting them aside to use
later adds flavor to my soups and vegetable dishes—it also
makes the pots easier to clean. The leftovers on the bottoms
of pots become new meals, rather than garbage in the sink.

Occasionally, I find someone willing to take on this practice
of shifting how they relate with food, willing to develop new

skills, new ways of working, new ways of using their bodies to care for food—for it is a body practice, something you do, and not just something you think about. It is one way of purifying your love, as there is no telling what you stand to gain from the practice. You do it because you decide to do it, because you are moved to do it. The effort comes from inside, largely unvalued by the outer world.

Often people make excuses. "We can afford it. Why bother?" "We don't waste food; it gets composted." "Nothing is ever truly wasted; it simply transforms into something else—eventually." Understood—we value our time and wish to make good use of it. While this may be true for food, the continent of plastic in the Pacific Ocean is growing larger and not going away in any of our lifetimes. Yet food is not just food. It is the blood, sweat, and tears of human endeavor as well as the burning of fossil fuel. With so much food these days, there is an energy deficit in that more calories of energy are used to get food to the table than there are calories in the food.

And food waste is incredible! I do not know how to summarize this, but I can direct you to feedingamerica.org, where you can begin to learn about this matter. Last year, the Feeding America network and its partners diverted over two billion pounds of safe, edible food that might otherwise have gone to waste, to Americans facing hunger. An estimated 25 to 40 percent of the food grown, processed, and transported in the United States will never be consumed.

Most people don't realize how much food they throw away every day, from uneaten leftovers to spoiled produce. According to the EPA, about 95 percent of the food we throw away ends up in landfills or combustion facilities. We disposed of more than 35 million tons of food waste in 2013 alone. In an article *The Atlantic* published in July 2016, "Why Americans Lead the World in Food Waste," I learned that "roughly 50 percent of all produce in the United States is thrown away—some 60 million tons (or $160 billion) worth of produce annually, an amount constituting one third of all foodstuffs."

Bottom-line thinking comes up with all the reasons that it's just not worth it to find ways to waste less food, whether it's the large amounts our culture neglects or the smaller ones at home. In the flow of all that is being consumed and disposed of, it is indeed a formidable challenge to consider what is *worth* saving and to undertake the necessary steps to waste less.

Usually when people do not scrape out the bottom of a pot, they also do not save two or three inches of leftover cereal. They may leave three or four inches of peanut butter at the bottom of a five-gallon barrel and then leave the barrel floating in a sink of soapy wash water to clean. I've also seen jars of peanut butter, honey, or jam discarded with an inch or more left at the bottom. Wasting less means forming an intention and then acting on it.

Making use of leftovers begins with not making them in the first place. Often, people cook way more than enough because they want to be sure of not running out. My aim is that we run out, just when people have enough to eat.

Sometimes providing too much food to eat begins with buying more than we can use. When I teach cooking classes, I really aim to make what we can eat. Still, people will buy more than the quantities I have ordered. To prepare it all, we then need to work extra hard to make extra food that we will not eat. So during the prep for class, I sometimes get out the scale: "Let's weigh this and use only what we are going to eat."

At home I don't have a menu for the week. I go through the refrigerator to see what needs to be used, and I use it. Almost no food is wasted. Soups often accept my offerings.

I also save plastic bags. At home I wash plastic bags and dry them, often on top of bottles on the floor. After they are dry, I fold them so that they fit neatly into other plastic bags that I can take with me when I go shopping. I estimate that I have saved fifteen bags a week, perhaps five hundred bags a year and five thousand bags in ten years, and I've been doing this for more than ten years, maybe twenty years now. Is it worth it? A particle of dirt on the summit of wholesome deeds, an offering, a ceremony—something I can actually do. See what you think.

What is precious is your capacity to find things, moments of your life, precious.

17

CULTIVATING A LIFE OF FEELING

In order to let go
of something, you have to
acknowledge it first. When
you do not acknowledge it,
that's called repression.

STEPHEN LEVINE

Real work surfaces emotions. Getting a meal on the table often means making a mess in the kitchen—one you may or may not be cleaning up as you go along. Not only will food cover pots and bowls but also emotions will spill and sometimes seethe. The results will not always come out the way you imagined they would. Cook's temperament often comes with the territory. Stress, anxiety, worry, frustration, annoyance, despair, dread—each another opportunity to mess up, mess around, clean up the mess, and eat it! How good is that? Making your messes edible. And on your better days, generating enthusiasm, joy, delight. It could happen.

Often schools of spiritual practice preach that when cooking, you should manifest only perfect love and equanimity so that the food does not convey negativity. I would never have cooked a single meal if held to this standard! In my school, learning to transform negativity in and out of the kitchen is what actually nourishes us.

Many have lost their way aiming for perfect composure. Donning their aprons of proper behavior, these cooks may become so stolid and sensitive to criticism that they are then unable to receive useful observations that could inform their cooking. To let in negative reviews may appear too risky, yet when we open up and sort through the verbiage, we may discover what is useful for stepping freshly on our own path, offering what we have to offer.

There are also cooks whose emotions erupt unpredictably. Something wild perpetually runs loose, and its would-be rider is unwilling or unable to acknowledge what is beneath the surface, waiting to be met and integrated. Gripped by the beast of emotion, the rider is being ridden. Taming becomes necessary: the rider learns to respect and value the energy from below, to meet what is in disarray, sorting out what is required and the way to proceed.

As Zen Master Hakuin says about the demons inside of us, who spend a great deal of time and energy battling with one another, "They were friends from the start." One aspect of working with emotions is studying and observing your emotional life to discover the choice points. The more you become aware of the moments when decisions are made—say, to be angry—the more likely you will make decisions consciously rather than unconsciously. Instead of an unconscious default stance of "this pisses me off and warrants anger," you will likely come to a place of acknowledging the anger and letting its expression go—"been there, done that, not today."

Another basic approach in Zen is to literally put your emotions to work. Instead of acting out your anger, by hitting something or throwing things, you put it to work, scrubbing the floor or washing the dishes, cutting or stir-frying the vegetables. You're in charge of how you manifest your emotions; you choose their expression. You fill your space with you, and you find yourself arriving home. You have a life of feeling, a life "in-formed" by feelings.

How to relate with our emotions is the work of a lifetime, or perhaps many lifetimes. Eventually, you chew and swallow and digest what has seemed completely unappetizing—and you are nourished. You make the changes that are being pointed out—altering the menu, the time to be spent, your basic stance.

A Cooking Class in Cleveland

In a restaurant kitchen in Cleveland, my cooking class was starting, and I began by welcoming people and letting them know that I was feeling anxious, nervous, and stressed. Working in an unfamiliar space with people I've never met can be disconcerting. During our prep time, I also discover that several of the ingredients were late arriving and that the promised ripe and juicy fresh tomatoes for a salad were instead orange and solid! I know that this is par for the course for time spent in the kitchen—making changes on the fly—but that doesn't mean that it is easy and effortless.

I let the group know I was stressed, that I was not as prepared as I would like to have been, "so please, be patient, if you would, while we work together and see what we can do with the circumstances we have before us."

When people hear this, they are of two minds: either they feel reassured, "Oh, if even an experienced chef gets stressed, then it must be okay for me to get stressed too"; or they respond the way a student who raised her hand in this particular class did, "Ed, you've been practicing Zen for over thirty years, and you're still getting stressed. What's your problem?"

Feeling ashamed—*Maybe I am a failure after thirty years as a Zen student!*—I needed to refocus as best I could. All those years sitting painfully cross-legged facing the wall, and I can still become anxious. *Oh no! What was I thinking? Guess I'm still a work in process.*

Perhaps this student believes that real Zen mastery means never having to experience any painful feelings ever again.

You've learned to be impassive or perhaps to rise above. No more anxiety, nervousness, fear. No more sorrow or sadness. No more disappointment or discouragement. You simply soar. You are unburdened. Your great enlightenment has changed everything. You're ready to be spotlessly serene—our mental image of Japanese Zen masters as strong, impassive, imperturbable.

I try to explain that I understand Zen differently, that I see it as knowing what you feel when you feel it, and that as you are informed by your feelings, you learn to work with them. Rather than eliminating or hiding your emotions, you aim to transform all that is afflictive into nourishment. If your aim is not to stress at all, you may need to stick to your comfort zone—repeating the same thing over and over! It will probably mean following a script rather than taking risks and being creative and will likely mean staying out of the kitchen. My aim is to *get real*, freshly meeting this moment for the first time, which it is, not knowing how things will turn out. Or is life simply about getting a good grade and passing through unscathed?

I am not aiming for peace and quiet and refined states of mind. I am intending we manifest a meal we can enjoy. Let's get to work. Let's feed and nourish. Let's cook! And work with all of it!

Using Emotions as an Excuse Not to Cook

Sometimes painful feelings become an excuse not to cook. Once, for instance, I was teaching at a Buddhist center where kitchen practice fell to the newest students—as all those more senior were busy doing "spiritual practices," including bowing, chanting, and visualization. Meanwhile, in the kitchen, we never knew if those assigned to work there would actually appear. When it was time to begin prepping the food, kitchen workers might or might not be present. Later, by bits and pieces, we might hear, "Oh, Lisa Marie (or Billy Bob) is having a kleśa attack." Technically, *kleśas* is a Sanskrit word for afflictive emotions. In this case, however, a kleśa attack translated into everyday speak meant, "I don't feel like coming to work in the kitchen today." With their absence, those of us in the kitchen felt less and less like working as well, yet we persevered.

I've decided to offer food, and I'm going to stand by my word. If negative feelings arise, we'll be conducting some negotiations. Am I going to do what the feelings tell me they want me to express, or will the feelings be coming with me to the kitchen and doing what I choose? Am I going to assist my anger to hit pillows or scream in the woods, or is the anger going to come with me to scrub potatoes and dice onions? If sadness is arising, am I going to go off and cry somewhere, or are the tears going to fall into the soup or the dishwater? Will they turn into the poetry of flavor and taste? To put emotions to work does not mean stuffing them, and it does not mean acting them out.

I decided not to let my painful feelings keep me from a life of benefiting others, a life of feeding others. I've chosen to cook, and that has meant working with what arises in the process.

~

A Workshop at Tassajara

About twenty years ago now, I was leading a cooking workshop for guests at Tassajara: "Cooking as a Spiritual Practice." My assistants had arranged tables on the porch of the dining room so that sixteen or eighteen of us could sit facing one another across an expanse of welcoming and reassuring red tablecloths. Sunlight sparkled in the foliage of the trees outside the screened-in area where we were gathered.

Again, as I had been in Cleveland, I was feeling anxious—this time because I had to change cabins at the last minute. The staff wanted me out of that cabin, ready or not. What this meant was that all of my things—books, papers, clothes, robes—had been put into pushcarts outside of my cabin. The white sheets draped over everything were meant to keep off the dust. Where were my class notes?

Though I tend to speak from inside during my classes rather than following a written script, I still find it comforting to have my notes at hand. Since they were not at hand, I began the workshop by confessing my anxiety and nervousness at being without my class notes. Before I knew what was happening, a woman on my right grasped my wrist and pulled my hand up toward her chest. "Are you feeling anxious?" she asked, paused, and then added, "Me too." My hand landed squarely between her breasts, where my right index finger snuggled against the softness of one and my little finger nuzzled the other.

What, I wondered, *is my hand doing between a woman's breasts here in the Tassajara dining room, with red table cloths spread out before us and the creek flowing by outside? This is a Zen practice center, after all!* Then I realized that her heart was beating quite solidly: thump-thump, thump-thump.

So I spoke to the room, "Wow! You're right; your heart is pounding away. You *are* anxious."

"I'll bet we all are," she said. "It's the beginning of the retreat."

Everyone laughed, and we all relaxed. Sharon Morrison and I have been friends ever since.

I was not being made less than in the name of extolling someone else's idea of a spiritual person, and I was not being shamed for being less than masterful. I was being met. We shared being human, and we acknowledged how sweet it is to share our hearts with one another rather than our judgments. When we allow emotions to do so, they connect us.

It's important for each of us, a soul incarnating into a human body, to learn how to fit in, to speak the language and eat the food, to dance the dance of our culture well enough not to stick out too badly. Our habit is to hide our emotions out of fear of being judged and rejected, but when we find those who acknowledge our emotions with warmth and simple presence, we relax. Not a problem after all.

When we are absorbed in performing well, the quiet voice in our heart goes unnoticed, while we stress over our reviews: What was my rating? How can I improve it? The voice of fitting in is loud and will tend to shout down the softer voices. If we are lucky, at some point we wonder about our inner life and about becoming more wholehearted, living from inside and expressing our inherent goodness. The choices we make—cooking or not cooking, eating out or eating in—then begin to come more from what is inside: I feel like cooking. I long to cook. I wish to cook. I will learn what I do not know.

<hr>

Being Cracked Open

When you are cooking, you are not just cooking: you are working on yourself; you are working on others. We keep studying until hindrances become the opportunity for practice.
SUZUKI ROSHI

Zen, we could say, is cultivating the art of having problems—"art" meaning to find out how to have problems in a useful, workable way. I say this knowing full well that few people appreciate the value of having any problems, let alone personal ones. So, being someone who is moody and intense, I appreciated Suzuki Roshi encouraging us to study how "hindrances can become the opportunity for practice."

Residential Zen training cracked me open—the calm, capable, centered young man fell apart, and emotions spilled forth. Practically speaking, though I was held in a safe environment, I had little direct help. You keep going and trust in the fundamental capacity of human lives to heal. Essentially, I was living a clean, healthy life—e.g., not exacerbating the difficulties with substance abuse or destructive relationships. I was also being as careful as I could not to act out or flood the room with my unresolved emotions. Even so, I was not always successful.

The Zen tradition largely emphasizes following the schedule and behaving with good manners. If you are having problems, keep sitting and keep them to yourself so that you do not disturb others. It's a steep path—following the schedule will surface troublesome emotions—and a wonderful container, yet there is no context for working with your emotions, for digesting them. You simply keep going.

When I was the tenzo at Tassajara, I got angry a lot, and I sensed that people often approached me as though peeking around the corner of a building: *What mood is he in?*

It takes a while to catch on that you yourself are the problem. One story concerns a monk who is angry because the wake-up bell disturbs his sleep. *This stinks!* he thinks. He's angry about having to get up, angry about putting on Japanese robes. He's angry about going to meditation, about chanting, cleaning, kitchen work: *Everything stinks!* Finally, during bath time in the afternoon, he realizes that he has a piece of shit on his face, right under his nose, and he washes his face. The world changes. He can smell the food again. What takes catching onto is that it's your responsibility to take yourself in hand. No one else can do it for you, as much as they may be walking on eggshells around you hoping to keep you contained.

It's not the pressure of the meal deadlines, it's not the misbehavior or incompetence of others, and it's not your lofty expectations of yourself. You've got some shit on your upper lip, and you need to wash your own face. Often that basic acknowledgment does most of the work. Once your face is washed, you may be sad, scared, anxious, nervous, helpless, and soon enough you realize, as many people have noted, that anger is never the first emotion. You've been unconsciously using anger as a cover all along, getting angry after your emotional stability has already been stolen by another emotion—drawing the arrow after the thief is gone.

Acting out our emotions makes little sense. Though it may temporarily relieve some inner tension to do so, the outward expression tends to become habitual, and the beast inside is ready to strike again later. You may harm your relationship with others as well.

My teachers and other students at the Zen Center often had advice on how to relate with emotions, which was basically to "Stop it." But they were rarely willing or able to examine carefully the details of how I was experiencing things. Don't express strong emotions—in principle it's fine, but in practice, when I was flooded with feelings, I was lost. Over the years, whenever I would become upset in the kitchen, others would tell me to "calm down" or "relax." By the time anyone said that, however, I would be ready to hit them. They had no idea. *Easy for you to say. You're not responsible for this whole endeavor.*

It was also frustrating that the people telling me to calm down or relax were not telling me how they felt (and I am often capable of a caring response). Had I heard, "Edward, excuse me, if I may: when you get angry like that, I feel scared and anxious." I could then realize, *Oh! okay, I better relax and calm down.* No, instead, they told me what to do so that they would not have to own their own difficult feelings. We've all got work to do.

One day when I was frustrated, someone confronted me differently, "Ed, what would you like me to do?" Very direct and straightforward. Right in my face! And in order to answer, I had to set aside my anger. I had to stop, pause, and recalibrate: What needs to happen here? I could ask for the assistance I need or take care of the needed activity. The anger was extra.

If I were starting to practice at today's Zen Center, I wouldn't last. I survived the rigors of cross-legged sitting meditation and an exhausting schedule because at the beginning we spent much of the day working, so I could absorb myself in the practice of cooking, connecting the fibers of my awareness with fingers and toes, with muscle and sinew, with bones. I studied by connecting this physical apparatus with the work of the day: washing grains, beans, and vegetables; cutting, chopping, slicing; cleaning counters, pots, pans, stoves, sinks, floors, walls, shelves.

I called it practicing Zen, here in America. I wasn't going to go to Japan and be subjected to their subjugation. I'd heard too many horror stories. Work was practice, and what made it practice was my willing participation and my connecting my awareness with my body and my body with the activities of the kitchen. I did not work with a sense of getting it over and done so as to progress to more important or more meaningful activities. Practicing in this way meant that long-buried hindrances came to the surface: anger, rage, fear, terror, sorrow, sadness, shame, disappointment, worry, uneasiness—in other words, emotions.

And following years of this "cleaning out the basement work," abiding deep friendship arises.

A curious phenomenon. Go wash your face, and see if there is something you can do to help.

＿＿＿

Sensing Essence

It helps to know that there is more to you than your feelings. One of my early experiences of this happened during lunch preparation one morning while I was the cook at Tassajara. Emotions swirled as I tried to track everything that needed to be accomplished to have lunch ready on time. Anxiety, irritation, annoyance—what increased the intensity of these feelings is that in the Zen tradition, meals are always on time.

When the bell rings, the food is served—which is, of course, not the same as, when the food is ready, the bell is rung.

Right in the midst of this sea of emotions, it seemed that someone was calling my name, "Ed." Perhaps it needed repeating to get past my steely but brittle concentration on preparing lunch. Also, the "Ed" being called was a most wonderful, loving, and wholesome person, while I was a storm of emotions. Who was being called? I was befuddled, at least momentarily. Could it be that I was the person being called? What was happening? Bewildered, I tentatively began looking around and discovered that Suzuki Roshi was standing in the doorway of the kitchen. Abruptly, the storm lifted, clearing without a trace, while energy sparkled up and down my spine. Bright light came from above. I was someone I had never met before, someone spacious and clear, someone blessed and holy.

This epitomizes a common teaching: you are not your emotions. Yet when emotions rage, the teaching goes out the window: you are flooded with feelings, and no other you can be found. So experiencing this you who is the sky is an important basis for confidence and moving forward. Though this was truly an important occurrence, I was still just at the beginning, and I've needed to continue studying for many years to establish a more developed sense of core, or essence, that does not vanish quite so readily under duress.

In Service to Something Big

There is a plethora of information about working with emotions, some of which I've found quite useful. For two or three years in the nineties, I apprenticed with an extraordinary hands-on healer, Lansing Barrett Gresham, and more recently, I have been attending classes with him again. I very much appreciate the care and precision with which he uses language, so if something here is not clear, it is my wording, not his.

Based on his study of science in addition to his hands-on experience, Lansing's sense is that as babies we feel what is in the room, whether our mom's sadness or our dad's anxiety. From time to time, intense emotions will be in the air, and as babies we feel! Remember that it's not until between three and four years old that we begin to differentiate "who is me" and "who is you" and what might be the source of a feeling—it's simply emotion in the air. Years ago, my next-door neighbor's young son once stood in the kitchen holding up his arms to his mom: "Pick you up. Pick you up," he pleaded, at this time before he could distinguish between himself and another.

Lacking even the capacity to identify the source of an emotion as other, as babies we're at the mercy of whatever is in the air, unable to diagnose the problem, let alone act to alleviate it. We come up with ways to manage the painful intensity of free-floating emotions. Our capacity to respond is much more limited than it will be later in life, when we have acquired many more options, such as speech or moving away from the disturbance.

Lansing's view is that in the absence of the emotional skills we may develop as adults, babies have three basic options—though, of course, babies are not consciously running down this list of options to make an informed decision. Babies can *crash,* which is to say shut down by going to sleep. They can also go *up and out,* which is to be above or outside the intense situation, and thirdly, they can *clamp down* on an emotion, or learn ways to internally shut off feelings. For adults, each of these options has a corollary. Instead of crashing, adults learn how to numb themselves. If our habit is up and out, we often find ways to get high, and if our habit is clamping down, we will look for ways to distract ourselves or to disconnect.

Learning to employ one or more of these options, we can avoid or turn down the volume of the feelings in a room. We relocate our consciousness so that it is not in proximity to the emotions that might be arising. Over time, we learn how to avoid feelings out of unconscious habit. To Lansing's three basic options, we can also add *going down* or *enduring.* There is also *aggression,* a kind of taking charge that often means not recognizing other.

Now the big question, the challenge that most of us face is whether we spend the rest of our life continuing to employ and reinforce these defenses—childhood decisions masquerading as adult choices—or whether we learn how to experience our emotions and discover how to be informed by them. Put another way, do we shift from being centered in our head to being centered in our heart, to our felt sense?

We often sense that we are choosing to guard the barricades to our feelings because the emotions are so messy, and we can become so reactive. In large measure, the world supports this approach, encouraging us to keep our emotions in check, either not to feel them at all or certainly not to act on them. Emotions, especially anger, can be scary. Any emotion that we are not accustomed to experiencing or that we lack the resources to cope with can feel overwhelming. We may then experience ourselves as completely engulfed, in the grip of the emotions, which we often experience as being helpless or out of control. And if we are out of control, what will happen?

Suzuki Roshi taught that "it is not so useful to spend the rest of your life hiding your weak point." Let's look at this more carefully, first by recognizing the potential value in acknowledging our emotions and then by clarifying the work of emotional tuning.

As babies we do the very best we can to learn how to be a human being in close proximity with others in our family. To get a grip on our emotions or a handle on how to control our experience is of such primary importance. Most of us manage this remarkably well, given our lack of experience and the limited options available to us as babies. Babies are learning so much about how to fit in and relate. It's later in life when we can choose to explore other possibilities, which takes us on what Joseph Campbell called "the hero's journey." In the Buddhist world, some call this "reincarnating into your own life." In her book *On Becoming an Alchemist*, Catherine MacCoun describes it as moving from the passenger's seat into the driver's seat. In Zen, this is also called freedom or liberation.

In an old Zen story, a monk asks his teacher, "How do I attain liberation?" The teacher responds, "Who is binding you?" My sense is that we each did this binding to ourselves long before we knew what we were doing. If you want to remain faithful to unconscious childhood decisions that allowed you to distance yourself from your emotions, you still have that option. But you can also choose to study yourself, your vehicle, and how to drive it, which means developing your capacity to experience emotions without reactivity and thereby clearing the ground of your being. You may then come to understand that you, as the sky, were never bound.

I would like to lay out for you my understanding of the world of emotions, and you can see whether it informs your thinking. After seventy years on planet Earth, I would say that emotions, far from being the great bugaboo, serve to help us cultivate intuition, connection, and relationship. What I would suggest, at least metaphorically, is that we have spiritual energy channels in our bodies, channels that can provide a flow of information connecting our core being, or true nature, downward with ground as well as upward to source. These channels connect our felt sense to our intention, to our heart and our head—a head that can go beyond believing it is in charge to relying on these interior connections to know how to proceed. But we do not realize these great resources are available to us because the energy channels are blocked by all the early emotions we put on hold inside us.

As the day unfolds, circumstances might well trigger the reconstellation of our two-year-old emotional body. These feelings can be intense—rage, shame, disappointment, desire—and they seem to be about today, but it is today's content associated with yesterday's emotions. Sometimes we sense this by noticing that our feelings are way out of scale with today's events. Inner work is necessary to clear out the emotional debris, so that our spiritual channels flow with clear energy. When our spiritual channels are clear, we sense our deeper connection with source and sustenance, by both sensing and knowing, and we respond intimately to today. Body, mind, and spirit are in the same place at the same time—often this is called *now*.

In Suzuki Roshi's words, we are realizing our true nature and learning to express ourselves fully. We "purify our love," which means that the spiritual channels within us are cleansed of outdated emotional debris.

There are many good resources for learning practices that clear emotional debris. The basic Buddhist sensibility is that one cultivates enough mental stability to be able to weather emotions in an internal atmosphere of mindfulness, not identifying an emotion as being you. Over time old emotional reactions are cleared: they are acknowledged and released.

Developing the capacity to notice and note an emotion without being captivated by it is essential for releasing it. Conversely, the more we act on an emotion as though it is real—and really about today—the more likely it is to recur and to continue to color our life and keep our energy channels clogged. Thich Nhat Hanh would use the image of "the storehouse consciousness," explaining that if you became angry, you must already have the seeds of anger in your storehouse, which someone "waters." When you react emotionally to an emotion, you recreate more of the same seeds, but if you can let the emotion pass through with awareness, you plant the seed of mindfulness instead.

As the channels become clear, you are more likely to experience things the way they are, rather than having them colored by your outmoded emotional response. Your heart of hearts was always precious, good, tender, and sweet, but when you looked inside, what was there often seemed disturbed and impulsive. So you kept thinking you needed to control yourself lest you bring harm to yourself or others.

While cleansing yourself of what is not truly you, you may become more and more aware that love and compassion are available. As Zen Master Dōgen says, "Guides and benefactors arise from the ground and descend from heaven." And you begin to discover that this flower of your life-force is flowing through you inwardly as well.

Of course, pretty quickly you will also realize that this flow of sweetness inside is not yours to own or appropriate, not subject to your control or exploitation, but simply something you can offer and share with others because that is what *it* longs to do. You find yourself in service to something Big.

You Mean It

You cook because you decide to cook. You decide to take it on and everything that comes with it. You cook because you mean it. Your heart and hands work more and more in alignment with your clear intention. You'll see it through because you decided to see it through—and because the work itself is making your love manifest. Food appears!

After Words

Full Circle

When your practice is calm and ordinary, everyday life itself is enlightenment.
SUZUKI ROSHI

Today I visited the bread bakery at Green Gulch Farm Zen Center and worked with Mick Sopko and Jeff Logan. There was a very sweet feeling in the room while we scaled the dough and shaped loaves to rise in baskets lined with cloth and dusted with flour. After they'd risen, the loaves were turned out onto a lightly dusted long-handled wooden shovel, and we slid them off onto one of the five shelves of the oven. After closing the door to a shelf, I had the job of pressing the pale green button that shoots steam in to make the surface crusty. The oven remained on all morning at 475 degrees, while we shoveled loaves in and shoveled loaves out and onto a four-layered wire cooling rack. We made magnificent artisan loaves of bread, including corn rye sourdough, walnut levain, rustic, poppyseed, and a new bread called "DNA," with more whole wheat flour than usual.

I was, it turned out, coming home, completing a circle that had begun when I was a ten-year-old eating my aunt's homemade bread in Falls Church, Virginia, and deciding that I would learn to bake bread and teach others to bake it. This vision initially came to life eleven years later at Tassajara, in 1966, when I was taught to make bread by Jim Vaughn and Ray Hurslander, who had learned to bake bread from Alan Hooker at The Ranch House restaurant in Ojai, California, who had learned to bake bread in Columbus, Ohio, after he says, "bottoming out from years of being a jazz musician."

Wandering the streets one day, he looked up and saw a small window in a gabled roof: "I'll live there," he decided and went up and knocked on the door. It was the Theosophical Society of Columbus, Ohio, and sure enough, he lived in that room for eight or ten years (or was it fourteen?). He found work in a bakery, and he also became enamored with Krishnamurti, who visited the Society. Alan eventually followed him to Ojai.

When we acknowledge our roots and receive their nourishment, they go way back. Sure enough, I passed on to others what I had learned in my book *The Tassajara Bread Book*, published in 1970. Curiously, as there were few other books about baking bread, it struck a chord and became a bestseller. Originally an enthusiastic offering from a beginning baker encouraging others to bring wheat flour, salt, and water alive, the book became part of a growing movement to bake bread that saw the arrival of dozens of artisan bakeries and one outstanding baking book after another.

Amazing. And now I am a humble supplicant being initiated into the ways of producing earthy heavenly breads, rustic or artisan, with crusty surfaces and soft interiors. Thank you to the warm hearts and able hands that have undertaken the task of baking these flavorful, nourishing breads.

Bowing In to Sacred Space

Spirits of earth, water, air and fire: Please protect this
bakery space. Help the bakers move with ease and grace.
Fill the breads we make with nourishment, good
flavor, and the seeds of awakening.

CHANT AT THE ALTAR FOR COMMENCING WORK
AT THE BAKERY AT GREEN GULCH FARM

Working with my friends, new and old, in this Zen bakery
space, I am charmed and reminded of so many things that
helped turn work into sacred activity: bowing and chanting to
begin, food offerings, wholehearted and sincere effort. Altars
help to dedicate space, to make the space larger, to invite spirit
in whatever form you choose. The bakery altar at Green Gulch
is whimsical. Yes, there is a photo of and a quote from Suzuki
Roshi on it:

> Bread is made from flour. How flour becomes bread
> when we put it in the oven was for Buddha the most
> important thing.
>
> In order to find out how dough became perfect
> bread, he made it over and over again, until he became
> quite successful. That was his practice . . .
>
> Anyway, we cannot keep still; we have to do
> something. So if you do something, you should be very
> observant, and careful, and alert.
>
> We should be interested in making bread that tastes
> and looks good! Actual practice is repeating over and
> over again until you find out how to become bread.
> There is no secret in our way. Just to practice zazen and
> put ourselves into the oven is our way.

You are making bread—and you are putting yourself in the oven! Good to know.

And on the altar, along with other cherished objects, there is also a wheat goddess made from corn husks that came from Mick's grandparents' village in Slovakia. We bow, we chant, we remember that our roots are deep, our inspiration is wide, we can offer our labor wholeheartedly with sincerity.

When you are sincere, you offer what you have to offer, making your best wholehearted effort—without hiding your faults or displaying them—and let others receive it as they will. An example of this is the Zen practice of preparing a Buddha Tray, tiny portions of food in small bowls, which is offered at the zendo altar before meals. As busy as I was when I was the cook at Tassajara, I found this custom frustrating and stressful: *I've got better things to do,* I would rage to myself. *What am I doing preparing dollhouse food out of a fairy tale?* About twenty years later, I realized how simple and brilliant this is. You put the food on the altar, bow, turn, and walk away. That's it! The Buddha does not say anything one way or another. Still, you make a sincere, wholehearted effort, offer it, bow, and walk away—that's it!. You've done your part!

In the great silence, you let others have whatever experience they have without trying to control their experience: some may like your offering, some may not. You're not in charge of their taste or their state of mind and body.

Wonderfully enough, your effort is acknowledged in a ceremony with a crescendo of drumming, while the food is presented at the altar—your effort, everyone's effort, the food, and all that has brought it to us. You give it back; you give the food back to the Vastness. May all beings be nourished—body, mind, and spirit, heart and soul.

Acknowledgments

The writing of this book has possibly been the most challenging project I have ever undertaken, as somehow it necessitated surfacing ancient disappointment, shame, fear, terror, and dread—however you might describe this: surfacing, acknowledging, letting go, reintegrating. The work of becoming a mature grown-up continues. Writing, then, is not just writing but finding a voice for the story. I've had to ask for help, over and over and over again.

First and foremost, I offer thanks and gratitude to my beloved Zen teacher Shunryu Suzuki Roshi, who took me into his lineage and into his heart. More than anyone's voice, his resonates throughout the book. Which means that the succession of Zen teachers is here with us.

Likewise I am indebted to my beloved teachers Dainin Katagiri Roshi and Kobun Chino Roshi, who tutored a rather intense young man into adulthood, doing whatever it took, whether holding my hand or setting me straight.

I have persevered with this writing for about fifteen years. While in many ways settled and stable, these years at the same time have been tumultuous—and at times painful for those in my near vicinity. Apologies along with prayers and blessings, my friends.

During this time a friend, Susan Piver, handed me her copy of *On Becoming an Alchemist* by Catherine MacCoun. The hair on my arms stood on end while reading the first page, and I read it through five times before I could put it down. (Others do not have the same experience: "Why'd you give me that book?") So thanks and gratitude, Susan, for this gift and for your abiding friendship.

Also blessings and gratitude to Catherine for her brilliant, humorous, down-to-earth, magical clarity, including an introduction to the language of *horizontal* and *vertical*. I proceeded to take several online courses with Catherine, including one titled Meditations on the Tarot, which further awakened my sense of the world being alive with consciousness. Another aspect of my voice. And she told me to get on with it!

Warmhearted gratitude for my next-door neighbors, Jennifer Buchanan and Mark Otavka. Your friendship has been a tremendous blessing in my life, including, of course, your introducing me to the energy work of Lynda Caesara.

I took Lynda's two-year energy class twice, with one year off in between. An extraordinary course—both times. Without crediting her directly, her voice speaks throughout this work. She and her students will be able to spot it. Thank you, dear teacher, for all the skills, tools, practices, and resources that you conveyed and continue to share. Living in sacred space—awesome!

Due to Lynda's recommendation, I managed to take a Process workshop with Myrna Martin. Over five days, eight of us—each with a full morning or afternoon's attention—went deeply into the realm of our womb experience, birth, and early childhood. With Myrna's steadfast, loving presence often reminding us to look around the room: the early trauma is not happening today! Thank you, Myrna—my gratitude.

Jack Elias, who teaches Finding True Magic (.com), and is an old friend from Tassajara in the sixties, has become a gifted hypnotherapist. After two sessions with him, I called to tell him, "It's like finding true magic." Thank you, dear friend. Love and blessings.

Over the last several years, I've had a number of sessions with Barry Auchettl that have consistently cleared my way forward. Signing up for his Master Mentoring course, I didn't follow up by becoming fabulously wealthy; instead, I finished my book! Thank you, Barry. "Practice gratitude," you said, and now I extend it to you!

Sojun Mel Weitsman gave me dharma entrustment in 1996 and has continued to be a trustworthy friend and mentor. More than anyone, for me, he embodies the spirit and practice of Suzuki Roshi. Let's continue this practice together forever.

Likewise I continue to be indebted and grateful for the teaching and friendship of Jack Kornfield at all those vipassana retreats so many years ago and at our way-too-infrequent meetings.

Moving on more specifically to the actual writing, I am especially grateful to Melvin McLeod, president and editor-in-chief of the *Lion's Roar* and *Buddhadharma* magazines. That he appreciated my writing, and told me so more than once, has as much as anything or anyone encouraged me to continue writing.

Kaz Tanahashi has been a gracious friend and mentor, as well as a prolific translator of writings of Zen Master Dōgen. The Dōgen quotes I've used throughout this book are from his work, primarily *Moon in a Dewdrop*.

Thanks to Jennifer Urban Brown of Shambhala Publications for working with me on *The Complete Tassajara Cookbook*.

Thanks to Jennifer Brown of Sounds True for reaching out to me more than once.

Thanks to Michael Katz, my book agent on more than one project, for being genuinely Michael.

Thanks to Caroline Pincus, my editor with Sounds True, for easing things along. How sweet is that? As well as Vesela Simic, my copy editor.

I am also in awe and inspired by the work of Robert Bly, not only his poetry but also his books *Iron John* and *The Sibling Society*. His live readings touched me deeply, and I have memorized several poems off of the tapes. My gratitude also for the work of Michael Meade, especially *The Water of Life*, as well as his live storytelling, and for the work of Coleman Barks, particularly *The Essential Rumi*, as well as his presence as a performer.

Grateful and delighted for my friendship with Haydn Reiss, as well as his wife, Zuhra, whose most recent movie, *Robert Bly: A Thousand Years of Joy*, is engaging, lively, and informative.

In 2005 Doris Dörrie approached me at Tassajara and inquired if I would like to make a movie on Dōgen's *Tenzo Kyōkun*, and I said, "Sure." We filmed the following year at Scheibbs in Austria and Tassajara in California, and the movie *How to Cook Your Life* premiered at the Berlin Film Festival in February 2007. Doris has a remarkable spirit, full of interest, curiosity, compassion, and playfulness. I am very grateful for her efforts, especially as her movie has inspired a career of teaching Zen and cooking courses in Austria, Germany, and Switzerland. A livelihood doing what I love, even though English is their second language!

Also, gratitude to Mathias at Scheibbs; to Shonen and Nakagawa Roshi at Zen Eisenbuch; to Arnim, Milo, and Rose, along with Vanja Palmers Roshi at Felsentor in Switzerland; and to Joanna, Sabine, and Edith of the Shambhala Center in Vienna—for all they do to make my workshops possible. I feel welcomed and appreciated. Thank you!

Here in California: Anna Thorn of Zen Center's Green Gulch Farm has appreciated my skills and invited me to work with her. Mick Sopko and Jeff Logan warmly welcomed me to a morning of working at the bakery there.

I am grateful to all the cooks, known and unknown, storied and nameless, doing what they can to offer food to themselves and others. In these acknowledgments, I'd like to focus on those I know (or knew) personally, offering my thanks and gratitude: to my mother, Anne; to my first teachers, Jim Vaughn and Ray Hurslander, mentoring me with ease and generosity; one of their teachers, Alan Hooker of The Ranch House restaurant in Ojai, California, who among other things sensed the possibilities for community and collaboration among his staff (and on three acres of California grassland built a restaurant and gardens); Alice Waters for her remarkable generosity, along with her profound love for the ingredients that move her, and for her devotion to her vision of the Edible Schoolyard (and so much more); for Deborah Madison, who practiced for twenty years at the Zen Center, then studied with Alice and subsequently started Greens Restaurant in San Francisco (where I worked), and her truly poetic sense for the ingredients and their possibilities; for Patty Unterman, owner of the Hayes Street Grill, for sparking my career teaching cooking classes with a one-paragraph mention in her "Dining Out" column; to Dick Graff, an unbelievably gracious mentor (and winemaker); and to my chef friend Robert Reynolds, as it is so charming to be greeted with two twenty-year-old Bordeaux wines upon arrival for dinner, along with fresh red radishes, sweet butter, salt, and mildly alcoholic French cidre—I couldn't be more grateful! Patrick Schmidt has been a complete joy to work with for my courses at Scheibbs—unbelievably professional. My special thanks and admiration to Charles Schumann, who takes me under his wing on my annual pilgrimage to his bar in Munich, Schumann's—great presence, along with simple yet beautiful food and drink. Also, my gratitude to Erik of Erik's, nearby in Eching, Germany, whose food is superb and in my price range.

I am thankful for Sharon Valentine, who lived next door for fourteen years, providing flower gardens and her warmhearted support for me being me as best as I could.

One of my students, Danny Parker, has put together a book of my lectures—to come out a year after this book—a labor of love, respect, and devotion. Though he lives in Florida, we talk on the phone almost every week to my joy and pleasure. Prayers and blessings, venerable friend.

Love and blessings to my daughter, Lichen, her husband, Scott, and my granddaughter, Danika.

Love and blessings to my precious partner, Margot, as well as thanks and gratitude for her dreaming up the book's title, *No Recipe*, and for contributing her artwork for the illustrations.

Again, thanks to Marj Stone for providing a writing studio at a rent I could afford.

JJ Cale and Leonard Cohen: not without you!

And to my readers: I believe in you.

Love and blessings,
Edward

About the Author

Edward Espe Brown is a Soto Zen Buddhist priest who frequently masquerades as an ordinary person. After six years of intensive Zen practice, he was ordained in 1971 by Shunryu Suzuki Roshi, who gave him the dharma name Jusan Kainei, which translates to "Longevity Mountain, Peaceful Sea." From May 1967 through September 1969, he was the founding chef (or *tenzo*) at the Tassajara Zen Mountain Center. His bestselling *The Tassajara Bread Book* was published in 1970.

After twenty years of residential Zen practice with the San Francisco Zen Center, which included four-and-a-half years working at Greens Restaurant as a busboy, waiter, cashier, host, wine buyer, and manager, he dropped out and moved to the woods above Inverness, California.

While earning a living teaching cooking classes, he did extensive vipassana retreat practice, workshops with Stephen Levine, as well as yoga and later qi gong practice.

Other books appeared from time to time: *Tassajara Cooking, The Tassajara Recipe Book,* and *Tomato Blessings and Radish Teachings* (which features both stories and recipes). He also edited *Not Always So*, a collection of Suzuki Roshi's lectures. Especially important for him was working with Deborah Madison on *The Greens Cookbook.*

Edward leads regular sitting groups and meditation retreats in Northern California and offers workshops throughout the United States and parts of Europe on a variety of subjects, including meditation and cooking, changing your handwriting, and mindful touch.

In 2007 Edward was the subject of a critically acclaimed feature-length documentary film entitled *How to Cook Your Life*, directed by well-known German filmmaker Doris Dörrie—which led to his teaching in Austria, Germany, and Switzerland.

He lives with his partner, Margot, in Fairfax, California. His daughter, Lichen, her husband, Scott, and their daughter, Danika, live nearby.

Inside he is a *sweetheart*.

About Sounds True

Sounds True is a multimedia publisher whose mission is to inspire and support personal transformation and spiritual awakening. Founded in 1985 and located in Boulder, Colorado, we work with many of the leading spiritual teachers, thinkers, healers, and visionary artists of our time. We strive with every title to preserve the essential "living wisdom" of the author or artist. It is our goal to create products that not only provide information to a reader or listener, but that also embody the quality of a wisdom transmission.

For those seeking genuine transformation, Sounds True is your trusted partner. At SoundsTrue.com you will find a wealth of free resources to support your journey, including exclusive weekly audio interviews, free downloads, interactive learning tools, and other special savings on all our titles.

To learn more, please visit SoundsTrue.com/freegifts or call us toll-free at 800.333.9185.

SOUNDS TRUE
many voices, one journey